Robert Mackintosh:
Theologian of Integrity

Alan P. F. Sell

Robert Mackintosh:
Theologian of Integrity

WIPF & STOCK · Eugene, Oregon

Wipf and Stock Publishers
199 W 8th Ave, Suite 3
Eugene, OR 97401

Robert Mackintosh
Theologian of Integrity
By Sell, Alan P.F.
Copyright©1977 by Sell, Alan P.F.
ISBN 13: 978-1-62032-425-7
Publication date 7/31/2012
Previously published by Peter Lang, 1977

ROBERT MACKINTOSH, M.A., D.D.

CONTENTS

	7
ations	9
: The life	11
e Presbyterian, 1858-1890	12
e Congregationalist, 1890-1933	21
terlude	37
: The thought	39
e Church and the Means of Grace	40
ilosophy and Theism	57
eology and Ethics	67
nclusion	83
x A: The Works of Dr. Mackintosh	85
x B: Some Further Words of Dr. Mackintosh	87
	91
Persons and Places	105

PREFACE

s book has been written for a variety of reasons. I wish to fill a gap in theo-
)iography by providing an account of an intrinsically interesting and intellec-
)urageous life. I wish to pay a personal act of homage to the theological col-
vhich Dr. Mackintosh gave such devoted and distinguished service, and in
much later, studied. But above all I wish to draw renewed attention to
osh's thought, for I am persuaded that some of his insights have permanent
and could well bear expression at the present juncture in theological and
cal debate.

names of many of those who have assisted me appear in the notes. Special
must be made, however, of the late Dr. M. Tandy, one of Dr. Mackintosh's
:s, who welcomed me to her home and supplied much useful information; and
surviving students of Dr. Mackintosh, whose reminiscences have helped one
er knew his subject personally to glimpse something of the man behind the
id articles.

Reverend Principal Edgar Jones gave me access to the library of The Con-
nal College, Manchester; the portals of The Congregational Library, Lon-
re thrown open to me by the late Mr. Bernard Honess; the staff of the British
Library gave valuable assistance on more than one occasion; and my col-
/Ir. Ivan Sidgreaves (Tutor Librarian) and his staff brought widely scattered
ls to my door. Another colleague, Mr. R.J Groves, of the Art and Design
ient, reproduced the photograph of Dr. Mackintosh from a copy kindly loaned
:ipal Jones. To all of these I express my thanks.

late Reverend Dr. W. Gordon Robinson, sometime Principal of Lancashire
lent College (subsequently The Northern Congregational College), who was at
Mackintosh's sole surviving tutorial colleague, read my work in its entirety,
le Reverend Principal C.S. Duthie of New College, London, and Dr. Lawrence
, Head of the Department of Religious Studies in which I serve. For their com-
nd encouragement I am deeply grateful.

n obliged to the editors of <u>The Journal of the United Reformed Church History</u>
<u>The Modern Churchman</u>, and <u>The Philosophical Journal</u> for permission to
naterial which they have accepted for publication. An abbreviated version of
two chapters of the book was delivered as a lecture to the Lancashire and
e Historic Society.

n greatly indebted to the Coward Trustees; to the Council of the United Re-
Church History Society; and to a number of individuals - including my parents
[r. and Mrs. C.A. Lloyd - for financial assistance towards the cost of pub-
his work.

I dedicate the book to my Mother and to the memory of my Father, who encouraged me to venture north to Lancashire Independent College.

Alan P.F. Sell

West Midlands College of Higher Education,
Walsall, March 1977

ABBREVIATIONS

Mackintosh's Books

:	Albrecht Ritschl and His School
:	Christianity and Sin
:	From Comte to Benjamin Kidd
:	Christian Ethics
:	Christ and the Jewish Law
:	Essays Towards a New Theology
:	A First Primer in Apologetics
:	Hegel and Hegelianism
:	Historic Theories of Atonement
:	The Insufficiency of Revivalism as a Religious System
:	The Obsoleteness of the Westminster Confession of Faith
:	Principal Rainy
:	Some Central Things
:	Thessalonians and Corinthians
:	Values

'nals etc.

:	The British Weekly
:	Congregational Quarterly
:	Congregational Year Book
:	The Expositor
:	The Expository Times
:	The Hibbert Journal
:	The Holborn Review
:	Mind
:	Proceedings of the International Congregational Council

PART ONE: THE LIFE

CHAPTER I

THE PRESBYTERIAN, 1858-1890

If it were deemed necessary to preface this biographical sketch with a text Robert Mackintosh's own words could hardly be bettered: "For one's own part would thankfully spend one's whole life till one was spent out, for the privilege removing a single obstacle from the path of hearts that are seeking God" (1). shall see, this was no mere declaration of policy on the part of a professional dent of Christian apologetics; it was the driving force of one who, although a was first and foremost a man of faith. Moreover, Mackintosh was a man whose had been hard won, and whose obstacles had not taken the form of those exter foes with which contemporary apologists loved to do battle - materialism, sce and the like. His difficulties were posed by the claims of his Church and the C of his fathers. This last clause is no poetic embellishment. Robert Mackintos born at Dunoon on May 23rd 1858, into a staunchly Calvinistic home, and nurt by Christians of the Free Church of Scotland to whom the Disruption of 1843 w crisis of their lives and the test of their loyalty. They, in turn, stood heir to tors whose line can be traced to still earlier troubled times (2).

Among those who suffered imprisonment for their faith in Covenanting tim Mrs. Lilias Campbell (née Dunbar) (3). Her daughter married John Calder, w came from Sutherlandshire, and became minister of Cawdor, Nairnshire, in Their son, sometime minister of Ardersier and Croy died in 1775 leaving thre all of whom were ministers. One of these was Charles Calder, minister of Ur (i.e. Ferintosh), Ross-shire, who died in 1812. He had married a Brodie, an second daughter, Anne, married Angus McIntosh, D.D., a native of Strathdea Inverness-shire. Angus McIntosh was ordained to the Gaelic chapel in Glasgo 1792 and translated to Tain in 1797, where he died in 1831 (4). Charles Calde Mackintosh, father of Robert, was his son, born at Tain on October 5th, 1806 Charles was educated at Tain Academy, whence he proceeded to King's Colleg Aberdeen, at the early age of eleven. After a four-year Arts course he pursue Divinity course at Glasgow. He was dogged by ill health, and spent enforced p of rest in Skye, Glasgow and London. Eventually, in 1828 he was ordained (5) in 1830 he returned to Tain to become his father's colleague and successor.

No doubt many factors contributed to the 1843 Disruption, including differe over ecclesiastical polity and theological emphasis. It must be stressed, howe that questions of church government and theology were not paramount. On the trary, as to the former, those who were to become the Free Church held firm the establishment principle - not least among them Charles Calder Mackintos As to theology, the impact of the higher criticism had yet to be felt, and on bo sides after the Disruption the doctrine of particular redemption was adhered t this last issue C.C. Mackintosh was, if anything, more liberal than some of h Disruption companions, for he was not averse to working with those whose wa stating the free offer of the gospel was inconsistent with hard-line particularit

lerlying cause of the Disruption - certainly in the view of those who felt com-
o "come out" - was the effectiveness of the 1840 evangelical revivals. These, claimed, showed the people what religion <u>could</u> be, and made them thoroughly ented with what they took to be the arid conventionalism of much of the shment. So great was the impact of revival in parts of the highlands that ple did not think of themselves as engaging in schism. As they themselves "The <u>Church</u> came out." That Charles Calder Mackintosh welcomed the , and was himself intensely evangelical in spirit, is clear from his own

"What I believe to be a genuine revival of religion, - the work of the Spirit of God, - has taken place during the past year, to a considerable extent in this parish and district. ... The experience which I had of the revival of religion, though limited and partial, is such as would lead me to long for its continuance, and to pant for its return, as bringing with it the blessed results for which a minister of Christ would desire to live and to die - the conversion of sinners, and the increasing consolation and edification of saints" (7).

last the Disruption occurred he stood firm, and was as a man from whom a had been lifted. The son of one of his elders, dispatched to the manse with the Disruption, arrived to find Dr. Mackintosh already in possession of a The Times. In the boy's own words:

"he patted my head and smiled; but such a smile! so full of radiant kindness. I was confounded, and as I went back between the hedges, the birds sang unheeded while I thought what could have come over the minister. Had anybody left him a fortune? or had he met one of the Shining Ones walking among the hollies in that early dawn? And it was not for some weeks that I found out that this was what had happened - the newspaper that morning had brought him the vote of the House of Commons finally refusing an inquiry into the affairs of the Scottish Church, and so making it certain that within a few weeks he would leave for ever the home, at the door of which I saw him, in which his father had dwelt before him, and which he would now have to leave without stipend, and not knowing what was before him. Of course, he came out" (8).

847 C.C. Mackintosh married Annie Brown, the second daughter of Robert of Fairlie, Ayrshire. They had seven children, Elsie, Eneas, Janie, Nan, Aileen and Jemima. C.C. Mackintosh's health continued to give cause for , and in 1854 the family moved to Dunoon, where he assumed somewhat lighter He resigned his charge just before his death on November 24th, 1868. C.C. :osh had not sought high office in the Church, and although his personality was l his friends were able to testify to his exemplary life and humility (9). At e of his father's death Robert Mackintosh was ten years of age.

I

Concerning Robert Mackintosh's early years it is impossible to be precise
may assume that he was reared in the customary Presbyterian piety of the tir
and from his own hand we have testimony to the effect that this piety was not
of irksomeness - at least as far as one of tender years was concerned: "I can
testify that one child, in his green unthinking youth, passionately and by instil
hated the psalm-tunes in the minor mode, of which he had to endure so many
made him melancholy" (10).

Shortly after C.C. Mackintosh's death his family migrated to Glasgow whe
they made their first, and happy, discovery of Alexander Whyte, then junior 1
of Free St. John's. They were later to come under his influence on moving to
burgh, whither Whyte soon went to succeed Dr. R.S. Candlish as minister of
St. George's (11). Among others who kept a kindly eye upon the widow with a
family to rear was Dr. Harry Rainy, father of Principal Robert Rainy and gre
uncle of Robert Mackintosh. To Rainy's home at Fairlie the family went for h
and whilst there were able to visit Robert's maternal grandparents, Mr. and
Brown, who lived nearby. The circle also included a Mr. Tennant and a cousi
Mrs. George Parker (12). By the time Mackintosh came to write his <u>Principa</u>
he could report, "The whole life of my Fairlie kindred and their other pious f
with (what we children thought) its almost too constant round of prayer meetin
passed away" (13). Dr. Harry Rainy spent his later years at 2, Woodside Pla
Glasgow, and Robert recalls his continuing solicitude for the Mackintosh fami
conspicuous support of the Moody revival of 1874, his conversations with Prir
John Caird, and his example of Christian hope and poise as death approached

It was from the Rainy household that nurse Emily Ramsay joined Mrs. Ma
Such comments as Robert later made about her are affectionate, and the pres
writer is informed by one of Dr. Mackintosh's daughters that he often referre
her. It was from her that he learned how her grandfather and another highland
danced before the Duke of Sutherland on the day Bonar Bridge was opened (15)
was in part by her that he was influenced, albeit negatively, in the direction o
long teetotalism. She would tease him for his clumsiness, and compare him u
favourably in this respect with his brother Eneas (16), but the overriding imp
is that the children found in their nurse a source of security and fun.

It was not long before Robert Mackintosh showed signs of that academic ca
which was to undergird his life's work. He won a scholarship to Oxford, but hi
mother declined to allow him to take it up, on grounds, it is thought, of his yc
fulness and of the remoteness of Oxford from Glasgow. Instead he attended the
versity of Glasgow from 1872-77, graduating with Honours of the First Class
Philosophy and Honours of the Second Class in Classics in 1878. This had ent
his attending courses and passing examinations in the following seven subjects
Latin (Professor George G. Ramsey), Greek (Professor Edmund L. Lushingto
1875; Richard C. Jebb thereafter), Logic and Rhetoric (Professor John Veitcl
Moral Philosophy (Professor Edward Caird), Mathematics (Professor Hugh B
burn), Natural Philosophy (Professor Sir William Thompson, later Lord Kelv
and English Literature (Professor John Nichol). Henry Jones was a distinguis

lder, contemporary of Mackintosh at Glasgow, and something of the compe-
irit over prizes (17) in Glasgow emerges in the latter's article, "My Experi-
1 Authorship" (18). There is no doubt that Mackintosh was more influenced by
Caird than by any other teacher at Glasgow. At first he endorsed Caird's
1; he later felt critical of it; but by the time he came to write From Comte
min Kidd (1899) he had reassessed the matter and was led to expound a
l idealism.

pears that with the passage of Robert from Glasgow to Edinburgh, where he
ead theology at New College, the family moved house too. Hence the family
with Dr. Whyte, of whom Mackintosh later wrote, "if I came through the
rs of youth and doubt without losing my hold upon the things that truly matter,
mainly, under God, to that one voice and to that one place" (19). Already,
re implied, Mackintosh was assailed by doubt. He was particularly exercised
eternity of punishment which was taught in the confessions of his Church.
ety became intense, and clamoured for expression, when he was invited to
a deacon of the church - a vocation requiring assent to credal formulae at
ation service. Whyte was sympathetic, and persuaded the young man that
were not saved by virtue of our belief in eternal punishment of the damned,
ubscription was less of an obstacle than he had thought. Thus Robert Mack-
as ordained deacon at Free St. George's. He owed much to his minister's
ig, to the Tuesday fellowship meetings, and especially to the great man's
l friendship: "There was for me a special charm in the fact that I never felt
l awkwardness in close talk with Whyte - he put himself so frankly, so
, so simply alongside one. With others it was different, shyness making me
ch" (20). We may surmise that when, some years afterwards, a letter of
from Dr. Whyte was read at Mackintosh's ordination to the Congregational
, the recipient was greatly cheered (21).

ert Mackintosh was placed second in the New College Entrance Bursary com-
and in his final year in college, 1881, was appointed Cunningham Fellow.
ction with this latter honour, the doubts with which he had earlier wrestled
ted themselves. He wondered whether he ought to accept the Fellowship when
o out of sympathy with the doctrinal position of its sponsors. He turned to
l Rainy for advice, and Rainy suggested that he accept the Fellowship, and
period of time afforded by it to think through his theological position.
osh persisted: 'Dr. Rainy, I don't wish to speak over-confidently, but I see
bility whatever of my returning to the old view of future punishment.' To
nade no reply. Looking back over many years, one sees that there might be
an one interpretation of his meaning" (22).

kintosh wrote little of his theological teachers (23), and nothing survives
st either that he approached any of them in general terms concerning his
s, or that any of them detected a troubled ordinand in need of counselling. He
npliment A.B. Davidson on being the one from whom students drew their in-
n, and brands the Professor of Doctrine (unnamed in context) "an arch-Cal-
ind one who loved to put a keen edge of paradox upon his statements of doc-
24). His rueful conclusion was that "we had no breath of modern theological

15

life in the system of doctrine taught us at New College, Edinburgh" (25). That
Mackintosh satisfied his teachers more than some of them appear to have sati[s]
him is evident from his graduation as Bachelor of Divinity.

II

The movements of Robert Mackintosh immediately following his departure
New College are not easy to trace. He pursued further studies in Jena and Ma[r]
though no documentary evidence of his residence in either place has come to l[i]
For a brief period he was a missionary assistant to Dr. Walter Smith, and du[ring]
this time he contracted scarlet fever. His mother went to Dundee to nurse him
also found herself serving as secretary to her son as he dictated notes which [were]
to form the basis of his first book. A recuperative trip to New Zealand followe[d]
and whilst at sea Mackintosh continued to write as far as he was able. Toward[s the]
end of 1883, and armed with an introductory letter by A.B. Bruce, he offered
manuscript to Messrs. Hodder and Stoughton. These publishers were by now n[ot]
too sure of Bruce's theological position, nor yet, apparently, of that of their o[wn]
reader, Professor Elmslie. After prevaricating, however, they wrote a letter
the author of which the following is an extract:

> "The subject being somewhat abstruse and lacking interest except
> for the initiated, we cannot expect scarcely a remunerative sale.
> However, as we like to be identified with works of ability, we shall
> have much pleasure in publishing your "Christ and Jewish Law"
> should you see your way to contribute, say, £40 towards the ex-
> penses of production and advertising.
> We should price the work we think at 6s." (26)

Mackintosh tried, and failed, to secure a loan from his mother on the strength
small inheritance shortly to fall due. When at last his funds arrived he procee[ded]
and Hodder published Christ and the Jewish Law in 1886. Dr. Marcus Dods re[viewed]
the book favourably in The Expositor, and to this Mackintosh later attributed t[he fact]
that his first book "came nearer achieving real success than perhaps anything
since done" (27). Principal Rainy, too, wrote him "a very kind letter of prais[e"].

The years in question saw visits to an uncle in the south of France, and a [trip to]
Palestine; indeed, as A.J. Grieve was later to remark, travel, "even by aero[plane]
was one of the delights of Mackintosh's life (29). But by far the most significa[nt]
feature of the interval of nine years which separated Mackintosh's leaving New [Col-]
lege and his ordination at Dumfries was the continuance of his spiritual quest [for a]
morally tolerable framework within which to exercise his life's work. In retro[spect]
he described himself at this period as "fighting for life as a Christian, and for [life]
as a preacher from the fetters of a seventeenth century creed" (30). This battl[e took]
an activist form in his rallying of support for the projected Declaratory Act. [Dr.]
Rainy was one of the main engineers of the Act, and he was held by many to be [swayed]
above all by political considerations: that is, by the necessity of bringing the F[ree]
Church into line with the United Presbyterian Church, in order that union migh[t]

itter Church had already, in 1879, modified its position vis à vis the West-
: Confession by passing a similar Act.) In fact, claims Mackintosh, behind
rt political necessity was a ground-swell of opinion which recognised the
a measure of doctrinal liberalisation:

> "I myself, ill affected towards the Confession of Faith, had got into
> touch with a band of younger men, theological students, who felt with
> unusual keenness the reluctance all students feel towards pledging
> themselves to the doctrine of former centuries. Our movement might
> have made little headway if we had not found support from Dr. Lindsay
> and the late Dr. James Candlish, who, among other things, were much
> swayed by this consideration. ... Ultimately, the official leaders
> took up the proposal, and it went through, on a modest scale, or with
> ambiguous results. To get into line with United Presbyterians was no
> doubt one motive. But it was neither the first nor the second motive at
> work" (31).

s the end of his life Mackintosh looked back upon the year 1887 as being a time
ny path in life seemed closing against me; and I tried to compose the turmoil
wn thoughts and beliefs by shaping out a set of what I termed 'Theological
ims' "(32). He did not publish these at the time, but that the discipline of
ing them was salutary we do not doubt. But it was not enough. "Milder
s of easing my passage of the barrier, constituted by the necessity of signing
stminster Confession of Faith, had failed me. I had recourse accordingly to
at violent methods; my mother, I now perceive, must have winced dreadful-
. He planned a series of "Creed Reform Tracts" of which two saw the light
The Obsoleteness of the Westminster Confession of Faith, and The Insuffi-
of Revivalism as a Religious System (34). He charges Puritanism with laps-
legalism, as a result of its stress on the duties of the Christian life, and
'-scrupulous delineation of those duties (35); he claims that the decay of the
cal way is the effect of the freer use of that very Bible upon which the old
had constructed its rigorist, logical, economy of salvation (36); he vilifies
ering Evangelicalism of his day for its exclusive concern with the salvation
oul: in other words, for its lack of social content and of a true understanding
octrine of the kingdom of God (37); and lest any of his readers should doubt
h types of Christianity exist he asserts, "my statement is not a caricature,
otograph, as faithful as I could make it. Such circles exist, - I have hardly
eathed any other atmosphere myself than that of the Evangelical party" (38).
ar, then, that Mackintosh's dis-ease with the Church of his fathers was not
attributable to conscientious scruple over confessional subscription, though
t this was of primary importance. He faulted his Church on its ethos, its
social vision, its tendency to make the evangelical conversion experience the
non of religious faith, and so on. He expresses this last conviction in an
ing way, with reference to baptism:

> "the Church's tradition is anti-individualist. Infant baptism is the great
> rock of offence to the triumphant revival. And infant baptism is what
> justifies a Christian, not of the revival species, in clinging as long as

> possible to the Free Church of Scotland, in regarding her as still a
> branch of Christ's Catholic Church, the mother of piety, and not a
> mere aggregate of saved individuals" (39).

We also detect here the zeal of the prophet rather than the animosity of the ico clast. He longed for his Church to claim the whole world - rather than the pio for the victorious God. "But, if not, God will do to us as he did to Shiloh. ... Headship of Christ is not to be honoured by shouting "The Disruption, the Dis as men in Jeremiah's time shouted "the Temple of the Lord." or "the Ark of venant" "(40).

For all that Mackintosh's dissatisfaction with his Church was many-sided overriding objection was, as we have indicated, that his Church was inviting h sons to make a dishonest, public profession of loyalty to a Confession whose v dity as an <u>unamendable</u> statement of Christian truth Mackintosh had come rad to question. The two following quotations make plain his attitude as the crisis life approached:

> "Oh, what an entrance is that to the service of Christ in His gospel,
> when one has to bow the neck of his reason to that which he cannot
> believe, - when one is deafened and dazzled with a dubious casuistry,
> till he knows not right from wrong, truth from error, what he holds
> from what he repudiates, and in despair submits, and steals in! Tho
> are not gates of righteousness which are so opened or so passed" (41

And again,

> "'Judge the tree by the root' is the ecclesiastic's cry all the world
> over; but Christ tests by the fruit - by what He calls fruit - and first
> and foremost by moral goodness. Many things are undesirable in
> one's Church connection. Only one thing is unlawful - personal sin;
> a lying pledge; a false profession. And that is what our wise Presby-
> terian Churches demand in the case of almost all thoughtful candidate
> for their ministry. Go where I may, I cannot secure that my neigh-
> bours have no motes in their eyes. I must secure that I have no beam
> in mine" (42).

How were the tracts received? Professor Elmslie, writing in the <u>British</u> implied that anyone who brought out two pamphlets at once was acting with unb ing immodesty; Dr. Dods, one of the most eminent (and non-revivalist) minis the day declared the second tract to be "a mistake"; and A.B. Bruce's cordia was confined to a personal letter (43). With the passage of the years, and wri from a less troubled vantage point, Mackintosh came to see that revivalism, v "in my fierce youth" he had weighed and found wanting, could nevertheless co stitute an imperfect method through which God condescended to work - though would still make conversion less absolute than the old evangelical theology ha it (44). However, whilst "I may have spoken with unseemly impetuosity ... w said sorely needed to be spoken - then" (45).

As to the remainder of the <u>Essays Towards a New Theology</u>, Bruce revie them, though not in a particularly helpful way as far as the author was concer

ne is struggling for one's life, if not as a man yet as a theologian, it is
the distinguished friend on the bank does not throw one a rope but rather
ie a push down" (46). The British Weekly gave a further push, with an anony-
irt review, and Mackintosh came to feel that "all these things were against
). His considered opinion was that more people in the Church agreed with
n came forward to say so, and that what they could not forgive was his frank-
3). Henry Drummond objectively summarised the situation in a letter to a
ated November 20th, 1889:

> "Mackintosh I know as an acquaintance of some years' standing. He
> studied for the Free Church, but stuck at the Confession and will not
> be ordained. He lives to expound the New Theology. He is one of the
> acutest minds in the country, a thorough scholar, and has already
> written one book ("Christ and the Jewish Law") and two pamphlets (one
> on the Confession, the other an attack on Revivalism). These pamphlets
> are too fierce. But his book is admirable. The new book ("Essays to-
> wards a New Theology") I have only glanced at. It is sure to be good" (49).

anwhile, Mackintosh himself had come to England. Still uncertain as to his
he was appointed to serve at Withington, Manchester, as assistant to the
erian minister there, the Reverend Benjamin Bell, B.D. His stipend was
a., and the appointment was for six months in the first instance. The follow-
: the period of service was extended to the end of 1890, but before the year
, Mackintosh had been ordained to the Congregational ministry at Dumfries.
rs that the reason for the appointment of an assistant to Bell (and Mackintosh
first) was the promotion of church extension work at Didsbury - work which
re fruit in the shape of St. Aidan's Presbyterian Church (50). Mackintosh
it stay, however; he would not make a lying pledge.

s impossible to say precisely when Mackintosh's thoughts began to turn to-
'ongregationalism. That he was favourably disposed towards that body is
om his pamphlet on revivalism, in which he speaks up for the Congrega-
ts against "the Anglican fancy that Congregationalists unchurch themselves"
hat cannot be gainsaid, since we have his personal testimony on it, is the
t with hindsight he described himself as "less ... a proselyte than ... a
" in respect of his new spiritual home. "I ... fled to Congregationalism,"
, "as a means of escape from outworn dogmas and creeds; but I resolved
i's help to be loyal still - or to be more loyal than ever - to the central faith
ospel ..." (52). All of which underlines the fact that the author of the pas-
certainty and doubt in A First Primer of Apologetics ("the only book of mine
as ever had the delightful words Second Edition inscribed on its title-page"
ote from the depths of his being:

> "Our young men, and probably even our thoughtful young women, must
> have their initiation into personal religious certainty through an ordeal
> of religious doubt. This is neither a thing to deprecate nor a thing to
> boast of. It is a natural appointment of God's providence, painful in it-
> self and full of dangers, but most salutary to those who face it with an
> honest and good heart. If we have never doubted, we can hardly help

the doubts of others - unless by a perfect miracle of sympathy and love; but most of us need personal initiation" (54).

CHAPTER II

THE CONGREGATIONALIST, 1890-1933

ert Mackintosh's own inititation complete, he found a haven within Congre-
ism, and on 11th December 1890 was ordained to the Christian ministry and
to the pastorate at Irving Street, Dumfries (55). The call had been addres-
im, in a letter dated 20th November, in the following terms (56):

"Dear Sir,
   At a meeting of Irving Street Congregational Church, Dumfries,
held on 18th inst. the following resolution was moved, seconded, and
agreed to -
   "That the Rev. Robert Mackintosh, M.A., B.D., be invited to become the pastor of this church, at a salary of £200 per annum,
   payable monthly, and that the deacons be authorised to sign a call
   on behalf of the church."
In accordance with this resolution we now hereby most heartily and
unanimously request you in name and behalf of the Church, to become
our pastor, on the monetary terms referred to.
   We have further to state that you will be allowed four Sundays each
year for holidays, during which the pulpit will be supplied and the expense borne by the church. We trust earnestly you may be led by the
great Head of the Church to accept this Call to labour among us, and
in answer to many prayers on this behalf, that you may come to us "in
the fullness of the blessing of the Gospel of Christ." May "He who
holdeth the stars in His right hand" guide your footsteps hither, that
under your pastorate His Church here may be "built up and edified"
and His Kingdom advanced.
   Assuring you of our very cordial co-operation in your work of the
Christian ministry in this town,
   We are, Dear Sir, Yours in the best of bonds,

   (Signed) Thomas Shortridge, R.A. Fotheringham, Thos.C. Farries,
       Samuel McLachlan, James Watt, W.M. Wright.
   Deacons of the Congregational Church, Dumfries.

November Mackintosh replied as follows:

"To the Irving Street Congregational Church, Dumfries.

Dear Brethren,
   I have received a letter signed by your deacons, and written by
your instructions, telling me of the Resolution by which I am invited
to become your pastor, and naming the salary which you attach to the
office, and the holidays which you offer yearly. I thank you for the
cordial and generous way in which you have received the candidature

of one, who, in several senses, came among you as a stranger, and having earnestly and prayerfully considered your call, I now accept it, trusting that God may enable us, so to live and think and work, in true Christian fellowship with each other, that we may unitedly grow the knowledge of His Will, and in capacity for serving His Cause. An therefore, I subscribe myself in words which I trust may be no empty form,

Your faithful servant in Christ Jesus,

(Signed) Robert Mackintosh."

An entry in the Church Minute Book, dated 11th December, 1890, records the tion of the new minister:

"The Rev. Robert Mackintosh, M.A., B.D., was this day ordained to the pastorate of the church. The Rev. James Gregory, of Augustine Church, Edinburgh, Chairman of the Congregational Union, presided The Rev. I. Hope Davidson, M.A., Portobello, read portions of Scripture. Rev. John Douglas, Glasgow, Secretary of the Congregational Union, offered prayer. Mr. Shortridge, senior deacon, read a statement by the church, indicating how they had been led to the choic of a pastor. The Rev. Mr. Mackintosh gave a statement of how he ha been brought into the ministry, and particularly to accept this pastor Rev. W. Douglas McKenzie, M.A., Morningside Church, Edinburgh, then, led in prayer, whilst the ministerial brethren joined in the layi on of hands. Rev. James Ross, Glasgow, thereafter addressed the members of the church, whilst Rev. Principal Simon (57), of Edinbur Theological Hall, gave the charge to the new pastor.

A Social meeting was held in the evening, at which Rev. Mr. Mack intosh presided, and addresses were delivered by Rev. Benjamin Bel Manchester, Rev. A. Fotheringham, Halifax, Rev. James Gregory, Edinburgh, Rev. Geo. Ure and I. Cairns, Dumfries. The choir sang several anthems, and Misses McKie and M. Irving contributed solos. The whole services passed off most successfully and were greatly en joyed by all.

R.P. Fotheringham, Secy."

Among those who sent greetings to the new pastor were Drs. Whyte and Rainy latter's letter was couched in somewhat enigmatic terms, and declared that M tosh was taking the right step "in the meantime" or "under present conditions'

Little is known of the Dumfries ministry. Mackintosh himself refers to th minister's club which met there. On once occasion he was asked to speak to th tion, "Can you entirely separate the State from religion?" He gave a negative and thus found the support of the Free Church ministers present, and the oppo of the United Presbyterians (59). This brief reference underlines the fact that Mackintosh was not prompted towards Congregationalism out of regard for the luntary principle.

It was at Dumfries that Robert Mackintosh met and married Mary Wilson

22

)24). Her father, a strict sabbatarian, was head of the English department
ries Academy. In later life in Manchester she performed a great deal of
ork, being especially interested in temperance work amongst women, and
ering a probation service in the city. In due course the Mackintosh's had
ghters and two sons. One of the latter was still born, and the other sub-
y, and to his father's not inconsiderable bewilderment, became an Anglican
:.

next firm date in the story is 15th July, 1894, under which the Dumfries
3ook records as follows:

"A Special Meeting of the members of the church was called at the close
of the morning service. Mr. Shortridge, Senior Deacon, took the chair,
and the Secretary read a letter from the Rev. Robert Mackintosh stating
that having accepted the appointment of Professor in Lancashire Independent College, Manchester, this carries with it the painful duty of
resigning from the pastorate of the church here.

The chairman then moved, seconded by Mr. Wright, that the resignation of Mr. Mackintosh be accepted with regret, but that the church
felt that an honour had been conferred on them, insomuch as their
pastor had been thought worthy to occupy such a position.

The Deacons then appointed a Committee of Supply during the
vacancy.

Thos. Shortridge."

Mackintosh's life's work was about to begin.

I

arrival in Manchester the Mackintosh family became members of the Withing-
;regational Church, whose minister at the time was the energetic C.H. Hick-
though Dr. Mackintosh was frequently invited to conduct worship in various
s, he nevertheless became a deacon of his home church. This office he held
death, though in later life he worshipped at Whaley Bridge, where his last
is. Mr. H.P. Griffiths, a lifelong member of the Withington church recalls
:kintosh was especially adept at talking to children - a not insignificant point
of his great erudition (60). He preached from full notes, in a rich, deliberate
d his prayers were invariably free prayers.

he College Mackintosh found himself a colleague of Dr. Caleb Scott (to whom
ated From Comte to Benjamin Kidd), and subsequently of Dr. Walter
:k Adeney, Dr. William Henry Bennett, "for whom he had a particular
and affection" (61), and Dr. Alexander James Grieve. To all of these he
alty incarnate" (62). The fact that he was never invited to become Principal
e wounded Mackintosh slightly; it is possible, however, that Mrs. Mackintosh
er more strongly on the point than he did, although they both recognised that
iot at his best when immersed in administrative duties. He was rewarded and

recognised in other ways, however. He had not long been in Manchester, and
but forty-one years of age when, in 1899, his first University, Glasgow, conf[erred]
its Honorary D.D. upon him (63). In the same year his <u>From Comte to Benjai[min]
Kidd</u> was published. In this book Mackintosh, who was by now reconsidering t[he]
Cairdian type of rationalism in which he had been nurtured, felt it in order to
against Kidd's disparagement of reason as a foundation stone of sociology. Tw[o]
points concerning this book are relevant to our present purpose. In the first p[lace]
we should note the searching review of the book by S. Ball (64). Referring to [what]
he takes to be a significant omission, Ball remarks, "he has not himself atter[npted]
to account for the evolution of morality; he scarcely suggests that there is an[y prob]
lem at all. It is, in fact, very difficult to extract a constructive theory of ethi[cs out]
of Dr. Mackintosh's book; his criticisms of evolutionary ethics are sufficient[ly]
shrewd and to the point: but the impression left on the reader is not merely th[at the]
application of the idea of development to ethical conceptions has been badly do[ne,]
but that it does not need to be done, or even does not admit of being done" (65)[. Ball]
notes further Dr. Mackintosh's implication to the effect that if we may not rel[y on]
evolution we must fall back on conscience informed by the Christian religion, [and]
says, "But till the authoritativeness and sufficiency of this guide is establishe[d, it]
remains a 'prejudice', and Dr. Mackintosh should either have made his point [of]
view valid, or kept it severely out of the argument" (66). Any dust raised by t[his]
review has long since settled. What matters is that Ball has been struck by fe[atures]
in Mackintosh's writing which were to be found in most of his work: brilliant a[nd]
penetrating critiques, flashes of real insight; but either too much humility (67[) or]
insufficient desire to be markedly constructive. As an old student put it after [his]
teacher's death,

> "He seemed to have almost too much reverence for the past masters
> of theology and philosophy. Although he criticized and interpreted su[ch]
> masters he nevertheless could seldom quite trust himself alone and i[n]
> the open, and felt most at home when he could quote the authority of
> great names for the views he advanced. This intellectual humility is
> evident in most of his later books. He seems in earlier chapters to b[e]
> gathering material and momentum for a final synthesis and original
> contribution to a subject - and then alas! to our surprise and disappo[int]
> ment the oncoming wave suddenly withdraws, casting up one or two
> fragments of tentative suggestion, in a brief closing chapter. For a
> signal example of this one might refer to his book, "Historic Theorie[s]
> of Atonement" "(68).

We shall see later that Mackintosh did not confine incisive criticism to his bo[oks.]

The second interesting feature of <u>From Comte to Benjamin Kidd</u> is the m[anner]
of its writing. It grew out of work its author was doing with his students, and [in the]
account he gives of the book's origin we have a useful glimpse of Mackintosh t[he]
teacher:

> "When I joined the staff of Lancashire Independent College, I tried to
> lecture freely from notes, following the example of Edward Caird.
> From the very first this caused trouble; and, towards the end of my

second session, I had a communication from next year's Senior Student to the effect that he and his fellows wanted me to fall into line with what (he declared) was the uniform custom at "Owens College", i.e., the University - dictating word for word. ... I indicated dissent.... But I had not got rid of trouble by persisting in my own choice. At the end of the current session the youngest member of next year's senior class brought to my door a letter signed by all five men "regretting" that they must "decline" to attend any more lectures of mine. I went to Principal Scott; he offered me no help; as he afterwards told me, an ineffective lecturer at Lancashire College had been got rid of years before in the same fashion, and he regarded my situation as hopeless. I next went to Dr. Goodrich, who sent me on to Dr. Mackennal; Prof. Wilkins, of the University, also interested himself in straightening things out. Finally, it was conceded that the Senior Year should have a class of a different order with me - submitting to me essays on selected subjects in Sociology; the men were told of this; and, after I had left the room, I believe they were warned that they had put themselves in a very perilous position by behaving as they had done.

Rather unexpectedly, this new system worked quite well. After a few weeks' experience the ablest man in the class reported to Principal Scott - who passed on the report to me - "we're having a very good time, Sir, with Prof. Mackintosh" "(69).

terial thus worked on became the basis of the book in question. In a footnote ccount of the above incident Mackintosh points out that in subsequent sessions rted to lecturing from notes, and it has to be confessed that he was not the fted of teachers - a point which requires support by the testimony of those ·ked with, or sat under him:

"Like other experts I think he knew too much to be a good teacher in the ordinary sense - an observation which I know will not be misunderstood by the discerning. His gifts were not of the "popular" order, whether in classroom or pulpit. That is no disparagement of him. But no one could sit at his feet without, as one of his students had said, and at least one of his colleagues can endorse, "being ashamed of his own dullness," and that is no small gain to the learner" (70).

e words of Principal Grieve we may add those of some of Mackintosh's stu- Firstly, John S. Richards:

"His students ... will ever acknowledge the debt they owe to him, but I do not think any of them could conscientiously praise his method of teaching. To put it bluntly he had no method at all. He simply appeared to be thinking aloud his own thoughts on the subject he was lecturing upon. He uttered detached, epigrammatic, always exquisitely phrased analyses, comments, and criticisms. You gathered what you could. As was said of Emerson's sentences, so of Mackintosh's, they illuminated the forest, but revealed no path. As cramming material for examination purposes such lectures were of little or no use. But

> merely to be in contact with a man so distinguished as scholar, thinker, critic, gentleman, and Christian, was of infinite worth ..."

Bernard G. Theobald wrote in more intimate terms in an article entitled "Mac Reminiscent," which appeared in the college magazine of Lancashire College:

> "Mac had no faintest idea of the art of teaching. He assumed that his pupils were as fully acquainted as he with the learning of the ages, and all they needed from him was acute criticism or commendation, as the case might be. Plodding painfully behind him and reading hard to cover our ignorance, we did at length get some inkling of the mean ing of his lectures and some insight into one of the finest minds in al the realms of British scholarship" (72).

Finally this, from one of his last students, Leonard H. Oldfield:

> "He used to lecture in the Senior Common Room, with the students sitting round the table, and his dog under it. Lectures were quite uneventful except when someone, accidentally, kicked the dog. They were not very interesting, and did not create enthusiasm for the subject. ... In the early days of my ministry, I found ... rather to my own surprise, how useful were the things I had learned from him" (7:

To his students Mackintosh was always "the Doctor" - except when he was earshot, when he became "Mac." His reflections upon his students would no d have made as interesting reading as theirs upon him! Unfortunately nothing of explicit nature exists, though perhaps the following recollection of another for student, James M. Calder, affords a clue:

> "Said Mac: "When Hegel speaks out he means that the idea of the oneness of God and man could never have got into the common mind without an historical incarnation. THEREFORE there was such an event; but it wasn't needed by philosophers - it was only needed by babes." The look in Mac's twinkling eye as he spoke those words left us in no doubt as to the category in which he placed his students!" (7:

II

In addition to teaching, preaching, and rearing his family, Dr. Mackintosl time to write. His efforts in this direction during the first decade of the centu amply demonstrate the breadth of his interests. We have already mentioned <u>A Primer of Apologetics</u> (1900), which book drew a cordial review from the edit <u>The Expository Times</u>: "Dr. Mackintosh's book tells us, more emphatically tl book we know, what Christian Evidence means today; and what it means today meant from the beginning" (75). The year 1903 saw the publication of <u>Hegel an Hegelianism</u>, which was hailed by the editor of the series in which it appeared as "one of the best volumes in the series" (77). The biographical sketch, <u>Prin Rainy</u>, which grew out of an article published in the <u>Holborn Review</u>, together miniscences which had appeared in Young Scotland, appeared in 1907. osh's friend, Andrew Melrose, published the book, but lost on it. With hind-ackintosh reflected that he had probably been insufficiently hagiological in unt of Rainy to whet the appetite of the book-buying public. However, "I yself to recall with comfort that the Manchester Guardian gave me a short n one of its centre pages, and praised my work. I may well mark the day of ae with a white stone" (78). The small, though wide-ranging manual, in Ethics followed in 1909, in a series edited by Principal Adeney, and then he most unexpected honour of my life" (79). Dr. Mackintosh was invited to ite articles on "Theism," "Theology," "Anthropomorphism," "Apologetics," osis," and "Dogma" to the eleventh edition of Encyclopaedia Britannica l). Since at the time Mackintosh felt most at home in theism's territory, he ticularly glad to have the commendation of Drs. Adeney and Peake (80) in re- his "Theology" article. An earnest of his later work in this latter field was cle on "The Fact of the Atonement," a finely balanced and movingly written nich more than stands the test of time, and is in the opinion of the present Mackintosh's most satisfying single paper (81). The contribution Mackintosh the third International Congregational Council (1908) further illustrates the g of his interests. His address on this occasion was entitled, "Recent Philo- nd Christian Doctrine," and in it he surveyed inter alia contemporary empi- pragmatism and idealism, in their respective bearings upon religion (82). sequent point in the assembly, Dr. Archibald Duff thanked "our masterly ckintosh," and added, "But I want to say, too, that some of us felt paralysed, ered" (83).

early years of the century saw numerous offerings from Mackintosh's hand eld of biblical studies. These range from short notes to full-length articles Expository Times and The Expositor (84), and also include a commentary, onians and Corinthians (1909) in the Westminster New Testament series y Dr. A.E. Garvie. At a later date he contributed "Galatians" to Peake's itary (1919). If the Encyclopaedia Britannica work was, in his view, the honour to befall him, the writing of commentaries "I felt ... to be the most il work I had ever known, and only wished that I had scholarship enough to my undertaking more of it, upon a larger scale" (85). The humility of a h!

ore turning from the field of biblical studies, it is worth noting that Dr. osh took part in the current public debate on the authority of the Bible. The lward Gough, B.A., Chairman of the Lancashire Congregational Union in ok as the theme of his Chairman's Address, "A Defence of Verbal Inspira- t the same assembly, Mackintosh, introducing discussion, denied that the riticism must inevitably have the effect of "blowing our infallible Bible to (86).

ology in Manchester at large was in the ascendant, and the several theolo- lleges in the city made significant contributions to the debate which preceded guration of the University's Faculty of Theology in 1904. In these discussions osh played a part, and, as he later wrote, "I may be pardoned for mention-

ing that I have myself from the first belonged to the Faculty as holding the pr(
though not lucrative position of Lecturer in what our University calls "Fundar
Ideas of Religion, including Natural Religion," i.e. - as other people are con
say - in Philosophy of Religion" (87). In a footnote he surmises that he owed l
appointment to the friendly initiative of Professor Samuel Alexander (88), the
sopher. The measure of respect in which he was held may be judged by the fa
he contributed a paper on "Evolution and the Doctrine of Sin" to the inaugural
ceedings of the Faculty (89); that he served as Dean of the Faculty; that he w:
summoned to teach Comparative Religion during two interregnums; and that a
semi-jubilee of the Faculty he was invited to give an address, Professor Peal
having recently died (90).

III

In addition to the customary flow of articles and reviews, including those
"Christians (names applied to)" and "Monolatry and Henotheism" in The Ency
paedia of Religion and Ethics (1915), the next decade saw the appearance of th
books from Dr. Mackintosh's pen. The first of these was Christianity and Sin
which appeared in the celebrated Duckworth "Studies in Theology" series, edi
that time by Professor Peake. Mackintosh pursued his theme through the Bibl
through history, and later commented, "The only apology I have to make for t
book is that I took very seriously the obligation to keep within the number of v
officially permitted, and that in consequence the diction - while not pure "tele
graphese" is often unduly curt" (91). Next came Albrecht Ritschl and His Schc
(1915), a book which was favourably reviewed in The Expository Times (92),
which also received general commendation from Dr. A.E. Garvie. Garvie, h
an authority on Ritschl did, however, feel that his own position in The Ritschl
Theology (1899) had been misunderstood by Dr. Mackintosh at certain points (
Finally, there was Historic Theories of Atonement (1920), which grew out of
Mackintosh's college work- which was by now weighted more on the theologic:
side than had been the case earlier. Although this was a typically cautious wo:
it was well received by no less a person than Dr. J. Vernon Bartlet (95).

That so much was accomplished during the critical days of the First Wor
says much for Mackintosh's ability to apply himself to his trade. He did much
besides. Mr. Hickling was succeeded in the Withington pastorate by the Rev.
Shepherd. He departed for Aberdeen in 1914, and at the height of the War the
Nathaniel Micklem (96) was ordained and inducted to the pastorate on 2nd July
The church had been destroyed by fire on November 22nd, 1914, and as if this
not enough to daunt a newly inducted minister, Mr. Micklem soon found that h
fist views were not at all approved of by some members of his flock. Mrs. M
intosh had espoused the pacifist cause, and whilst the reverse was true of Dr.
Mackintosh, he stood by his minister's right to his convictions, and gave the :
lems hospitality in his home after their minister had resigned the pastorate.

If any in Lancashire were in any doubt as to Mackintosh's own views on tl
pacifist-non-pacifist issue, they were without excuse after his Address from

the Lancashire Congregational Union, which he held in 1918. The following tract from the <u>Year Book</u> of that Union:

"After a devotional service conducted in the absence of Rev. H. Partington M.A., by Rev. A. Pickles M.A. the hall was well filled for the Address from the Chair. The subject was 'The State'; the treatment being dominated throughout by the international situation. With his usual thoroughness and incisiveness Dr. Mackintosh did not hesitate to carry the authority he claimed for the State to its logical - and absolute - conclusions. Law and order, justice and right must be maintained between nations as between individuals, even though the shining sword of the State - a weapon meant to be used - had to be stained with blood. We must 'endure to the end' that civilisation and right might be saved.

The address, 'a thorough war aims pronouncement,' was welcomed with enthusiasm by the 'warriors' of the Assembly, while the 'pacifists' listened with commendable patience, although one of them protested that the sentiments should not go forth to the world as the considered opinion of the Union.

Discussion, impossible in the Assembly, broke out over the luncheon tables. Dr. Mackintosh had certainly livened us up, and, although there were different opinions about the usefulness to ministers and churches of such a controversial address, it was agreed that, from its point of view the case could not have been better put. Altogether, the difference of view reminded us of the scene described in Ezra, when the foundation of the new Temple was laid: - "Many wept with a loud voice, and many shouted aloud for joy, so that the people could not discern the noise of the shout for joy from the noise of weeping," only in our case some of the old men rejoiced and some of the young wept" (97).

Chair of the Lancashire Union marked Dr. Mackintosh's peak of attainment ʰhly office. As Dr. Grieve was later to remark, the loved and honoured osh was "A man whose heart and mind, saintliness and scholarship, Congre- ism too largely overlooked: it would have honoured itself indeed in calling he Chair of the Union" (98).

IV

920 Dr. Mackintosh was one of the English representatives to the Interna- ongregational Council meetings at Boston, Mass. One of his daughters recalls ght with which he embarked upon this mission, and the pleasure with which looked back upon his visit. At the Council, in the absence through ill health ʔ.T. Forsyth, he introduced the Report of the Commission on "The Contri- f British Congregationalism to Religious Thought," on which he had served. ddress he ranged widely, the question of the application of theological in- ɔ social questions receiving a fair amount of attention. This latter concern ɔh in his mind when, in 1924, he attended the COPEC (99) conference at

Birmingham. He felt keenly that the tone of the papers presented was such as blunt the dogmatic edge of Christianity. Indeed, he later described the confer as "an assemblage of warm young hearts and hot young heads" (100). Mackint had no quarrel with the desire of the speakers to serve mankind, but he conte that in a number of directions dangerous notes were being struck. For examp he suspected the commission reporters of undue sacramentalism. Concernin: Jesus's method of moving from nature parables to religious truth, the report "It was as they came to see the God whose nature and operations they had bee tracing in the mustard-seed ... supremely revealed as incarnate in their Ma that their whole personalities were saturated by the inflowing of the Divine" (But were they similarly saturated by the contemplations of unrighteous judges such as these appear in the parables too. "The discovery of ideal beauty in th world is too weak an argument to efface the reiterated impression of nature's difference, still more to disprove nature's apparent cruelty" (102). More ser

> "A grave issue is raised when we are told that revelation is 'given through the medium (1) of the material,' and only (2) of the personal." ... I am inclined to submit that God's action, whether in revelation or in grace, is personal 'first, second, and all the time,' and that the opposite view would legitimate gross belief in magic" (1

The whole of Dr. Mackintosh's protest was in the interest of his evangelical u standing of the grace of God. A final quotation will amply make the point:

> "According to the Report, 'The word redemption sums up our best conception of God's purpose for the world, its <u>gradual approximatior</u> to the Divine idea.' So again, we are to '<u>carry on</u> Christ's redempti\ work,' and are 'dedicated for the <u>continuance</u> of His redemptive worl But, in the language of faith,
> 'Love's redeeming work is done,
> Fought the fight, the battle won'." (104)

So, at the end, Mackintosh asks, "Do readers who share the evangelical loyal regard the COPEC statements as adequate or safe" (105)? It may be that in c Mackintosh underestimated the role of the Church <u>qua</u> body of Christ as being agent of the Lord's business in the world. But with the emphasis going all the way this may be forgiven. Certainly it would seem that careless talk about th Church as being the continuation of the Incarnation can remove the note of "or for all" from the Church's message. And many would say that without that not is no gospel, and therefore no Church. Reflecting later upon the events of CO Mackintosh privately said that by his intervention he had saved the Conference following the Quakers; and Dr. Grieve, in his funeral oration, particularly r the occasion of the COPEC Conference, when Mackintosh "saved that assembl committing itself in a moment of emotional economics to a fatal slough" (106)

In the same year as COPEC, 1924, Mrs. Mackintosh died. By now the ch were growing up and had gone away to further their education. The surviving entered Ridley Hall and became an Anglican minister; one of the daughters be a Quaker - two occurrences which, if they did not shake Dr. Mackintosh, did puzzle him. He engrossed himself in the work of various societies. He was s ocal auxiliary of the British and Foreign Bible Society, and a director of the Missionary Society. In this latter role, "His interventions in discussion frequent, and were generally designed to pour a douche of cold water on ticable proposals or sentimental moods. His pet aversion was sloppiness in phases" (107). Mackintosh served as a governor of the John Rylands Library, ster, and was a highly respected member of a united ministers' fraternal, he Manchester Congregational Board and Ministers' Board. In this last con- "he seldom failed to open the discussion, and not rarely to leave little to be 108). Finally, as deacon at Withington, he gave wise guidance as the rebuild- he church was planned. The new building was opened on 17th October, 1925 - after the tragic death by drowning of the minister who had led the project, . Joseph Ferguson, and his daughter Joan. The accident had occurred at ith, and the new church building contained memorial windows to minister ghter. For a summary statement indicative of the seriousness with which tosh took his committee work we may turn to Rev. George Phillips: "if the was absent from a meeting, of which he had been duly notified, it was cer- her that he was ill or that the tram had broken down" (109).

. Mackintosh continued to write: in particular a large number of articles and ; for the then youthful but now lamented Congregational Quarterly (110). He the arena of public debate, through the columns of the Manchester Guardian, nterest of anti-sacramentarian, evangelical Christianity; and he contributed rief articles to the fourteenth edition of Encyclopaedia Britannica (1929). On asion the larger themes had been "entrusted to more conspicuous writers. ideavoured to sparkle in my remaining half columns, according to instruc- eceived" (111).

o books remain to be noted. Values (1928) was greeted by The Expository as "a book of modest dimensions but of very great excellence ..." (112), . T.S. James accorded the book high praise, and said "I can think now of r fortune befalling some of our modernists than to get in the cross-fire of ckintosh's criticisms" (113). In this book, published at his own expense (114), tosh spoke inter alia of economic, pleasure, pragmatic and metaphysical and sought to relate them to religious values. He concluded that salvation ighest of all values "in which every minor value will find its due place, or ch - if need arises - many a minor value may be joyfully surrendered in of that 'one pearl of great price' "(115).

. Mackintosh's last book, Some Central Things, was published in 1932. Here e of Jesus Christ as the fulfiller of the messianic expectation, whose ministry i apparent defeat, not because he lost personal popularity, but because, for t part, his hearers "repented not" (116).

now Mackintosh had retired from his post at Lancashire College, and had iome at Whaley Bridge. June 1930 saw the end of his distinguished profes- areer, and the occasion was well marked. At the Annual Meeting of the Col- 20th June distinguished guests included Professor Samuel Alexander and berly, the Vice Chancellor of the University. The following extract from ichester Guardian report of the proceedings adequately conveys the spirit of asion:

"At the business meeting which preceeded the public meeting a strikingly-worded resolution referring to Dr. Mackintosh's work was passed, the concluding words of which were: 'If to-day, with sorrow, we note the completion of a great ministry, we assure the reverend professor that he can never be separated from the College to which he has given his life. What he has done sets itself for ever amongst the powerful, unseen things in which the wealth of the College must ever be found. In the days which, it is our prayer, may yet be granted him, we hope that he will know that he is surrounded by the grateful remembrance of the men and women he has taught, and the honour of the College to which he has added permanent strength and distinction.'

At the public meeting Dr. Mackintosh was presented with a cheque for 200 guineas and an illuminated address, and the Rev. B.G. Theobald, the Rev. W.E. Harding, and Dr. Moberly spoke in high praise of his work and character. Dr. Moberly said that Dr. Mackintosh's connection with the University was not quite so long as his connection with the College, because the Faculty of Theology at the University, with which Dr. Mackintosh was associated, only came into existence 26 years ago. Dr. Mackintosh was, however, the one surviving active member of those who started that Faculty, and throughout the 26 years he had served it not only with self-sacrificing energy but with a robust fearlessness which enabled a man always to speak of that which he himself had seen and known and held with conviction. During all that time Dr. Mackintosh had been responsible for the teaching in the University of the philosophy of religion - the most difficult and the most profound subject that the human mind could study.

Dr. Mackintosh in reply, said that if he could offer a word of personal spiritual advice to those who were students at the College, it was that they must always have an edge on their intellect and spirit.

'Unless you keep that edge bright,' he said, 'you are preparing for certain disappointment. A C3 Christian who takes upon himself or herself the tasks of the ministry is preparing for a future of bitter disappointment that is not likely to be confined to the person most immediately responsible.' As compared with former generations he thought the present generation was keenly alive to the necessity of the cultivation of a devotional life" (117).

V

In 1932 Dr. Mackintosh's health began to decline, and his last public appearances were made on January 23rd, 1933. On the morning of that day he attend meeting of the College Committee, and in the afternoon, a meeting of the Ryla

Committee. After evening prayers in the college chapel he suffered a heart
He spent a week in college, and was then moved home to Whaley Bridge. An
)n in Manchester was called for, which he just survived; but on Sunday,
·y 12th, 1933, Dr. Mackintosh died. On the Wednesday the funeral service
d at the College, and this was followed by interment at Taxal churchyard (118).

: funeral service opened with the metrical version of Psalm 23. Dr. Grieve
: scriptures and delivered the oration. Professor Murphy offered prayer,
r the hymn, "O God of Bethel," the Reverend T.T. James (who had entered
as a student in Dr. Mackintosh's first year as Professor) pronounced the
tion. Dr. Grieve and the Revs. H.H. Orme and H. Partington officiated at
reside.

v shall we appraise Dr. Mackintosh, the man? If it is difficult to judge the
er of a person long since dead, it is doubly hard to assess adequately one
·emembered by some, though not by the writer. We shall do well to be guided
eflections of those who knew him, and to trust that the resulting impression
)o wide of the mark.

)ert Mackintosh was a gracious father, who brought his family up to keep the
Day. On Sundays the games played in the Mackintosh household differed from
tjoyed on other days, and included Bible ludo. Daily family prayers were
iry for all until the children went to school, when weekly family worship on
replaced them. Though by no means cold towards his children, they tended
more contact with their mother, and often learned their father's mind
her.

sic was among Dr. Mackintosh's extra-mural interests. Although he played
uments he had a fine baritone voice, loved singing, and enjoyed the concerts
allé orchestra. In his younger days he was a keen cyclist. A daughter is
c that gardening did not fall within his purview!

have already described the reactions of some of Mackintosh's students to
hing. It may be that the following further extracts will go some way towards
ing a more rounded picture of their mentor:

> "I have often recalled, for my own good, hearing him preach in the
> Chorlton Road Church; what he said that morning has long since
> passed from my mind, but not the Text, Jeremiah 45.5: "Seekest
> thou great things for thyself? Seek them not." And I realised that
> this was true of the man himself. He neither looked for nor sought
> the praise of men; his walk was close with God, and he was always
> faithful to the Truth as it had been revealed to him. He had no use
> for small talk, but was no pedant. I think he was a shy man, at
> times he even appeared to be aloof; but to be in his company was
> to be enlarged, to listen to him speak his thoughts was to be prompted
> to set out in quest for Truth as it is in Christ Jesus, and always to
> be enlightened. He had that natural dignity which belongs to greatness,
> but it was shot through with a Humility Kindness and Grace, which
> are the sure indications of real Sanctity.

Outside of academic life, there are just two recollections of him which I would like to mention, each of them for me indicative of his kindness and largeness of heart. He loved music; and I remember well how on one occasion in his home, when a number of us were enjoying a social evening with him and his truly charming wife, I had sung Henley's "Invictus." He placed his hand on my shoulder and remarked, "Thank you Wilson, that was indeed a truly elegant expression of paganism." And how can I ever forget how on the occasion of my Ordination, he made the long journey from Manchester to Hartlepool to pray for me and so strengthened my hand in the hand of God. For me the very thought of "Mac" is not only an honoured Memory, it is a hallowed one" (119).

"I know only one word comprehensive enough to describe his fascinating personality. It is gravitas shot through and through with Grace. To be in his presence was to be conscious of his authority. To talk with him was to feel oneself a larger man. To have the luck of sharing his thinking was to fall in love with truth. His dignity was that of a man who walked humbly with God. It was "Mac" who comforted me most when my mother died. At the graveside in Manchester he turned to me and said, "Your father will need you quite specially now." His words killed self-pity and dried my tears and gave me strength" (120).

"Like many others, I had always been apprehensive when on the Theolog. table I found the only vacant seat at breakfast or dinner was next to him, for one's most valiant effort at conversation - some news item, a new book, or what not - seldom produced any rejoinder other than, "Really", "Is that so?", or what one felt to be equally squelching. I felt later that this was ... his habitual mental reserve, weighing whatever minute facts might have been presented to him. ... The one and only time I ever preached to him, when I supplied at Marple Bridge in my senior year and he was in the congregation to my consternation, ... he thanked me for my 'ministration this morning', adding, 'I greatly appreciated the Benediction'. I still wonder if that was in relief that I had got to the end. But he was not capable of satire. ..." (121).

"He sought to live his life: -
   "As ever in my great Taskmaster's eye."
   This great principle was applied not only to the big and important, but also to the most insignificant matters of conduct, and often took the form of meticulous truthfulness. There is preserved at the College an envelope which he had addressed to the Principal and marked "Urgent." This, appearing on reconsideration rather too strong an expression, he had crossed out and substituted, "Tolerably urgent." He was too truthful ever to be lavish in praises. A student whose sermon was summed up by him as "not altogether unhelpful" had cause for much satisfaction.

All the obituary notices I have read so far have made some
reference to his "austerity," or his "unapproachableness." It is of
course true that he could not easily fraternise, but the impression
of aloofness was very deceptive. Actually he was a kindly, genial
soul who loved good company, and the delights of conversation and
society. He had a keen sense of humour. ... The idea that he was
an ascetic or a recluse is quite mistaken. In his prayers he would
often praise the Goodness which has "given us richly all things to
enjoy."

Furthermore it is true that as a critic, and especially in debate,
where I think his marvellous analytical powers were displayed to
their best advantage, he could be devastating. His intellect was a
sword with point like a needle and edges keen as a razor. And his
command of English was such that it cut and penetrated with a
maximum of power and precision. And there can be no sort of
doubt but that he revelled in dealing with bad logic, and exposing
fallible propositions. But if he discovered that he had hurt anyone's
feelings he was keenly distressed. "I hope," he apologised to me
one morning after an exceptionally brilliant and desolating onslaught
upon a paper of mine, "you didn't think me too slashing this morning?" "Doctor," I answered, "You wouldn't be yourself if you
weren't slashing. We expect it of you!" He didn't smile. He looked
at me in pained surprise, and the shake of his head meant without
question: "Is that the sort of man I'm supposed to be?"

But with all his intellectual eminence he was in spirit profoundly simple and humble ... though he was conversant with all the
highways and by-ways of philosophic doubt he lived and died, as
the lowliest of Christ's followers, simply trusting in the redeeming mercy and grace which we have in Him" (122).

may fittingly conclude this section of our work by reproducing some further
s from Dr. Grieve's funeral oration:

"I have never known a man who had a stronger sense of duty ...
I have never known a man who had stronger convictions ... It was
no light thing for him to break with the church of his fathers. ...
But when the decision was made he never wavered. ...

I have never known a man more free from guile, to whom everything mean and petty and ignoble was utterly foreign. ...

His invariable courtesy is a precious inheritance to all who
knew him; it had its own peculiar quality in virtue of a certain
reserve which even had a semblance of austerity. ...

He could be excited, he could be vehement, but he was never
flurried ...

In the College itself we best appreciated him when he took part
in the services of our sanctuary and especially for the addresses
which, in his turn, he delivered at the beginning of term. Alongside these I should set the charges he gave to students at their
ordination.

In prayer he had the gracious power of bringing us into the secret place of the Most High as one whose joyous privilege it was to dwell in the presence of God. His knowledge of Scripture was matched by his acquaintance with the devotional literature and hymnology of the ages ...

Two distinct tendencies or temperaments met in him. He had the mind of a man, the heart of a child. On the one hand there was a very simple religion, "old fashioned" if you like. I have heard him tell a company of people how he owed his second birth to Moody and Sankey, and one of his favourite sermons was on the story of the Prodigal Son. On the other hand there was a restless, enquiring, critical mind that subjected every proposition to remorseless scrutiny and despised the way of easy compromise. The two were inevitably in conflict from time to time. But if he had his hours of doubt he had also his hours of victory.

We have seen him deal mercilessly with weak points in a speech or paper to which he had listened. ... But we have seen him also binding up the wounds, administering the cordials, and giving strength to those who had no might" (123).

INTERLUDE

now come to a more detailed consideration of Dr. Mackintosh's thought.
of his critical as over against his constructive strength, we shall have to
l ideas and suggestions culled from the whole span of his work. What he
id for himself we must attempt to do for him, confident that much of real
ill emerge. Our objective cannot, however, be exhaustiveness. Since some
sues with which he dealt are long since dormant, we shall for the most
centrate upon those matters which have particular relevance to Dr.
osh's life, and upon those of which the Church of the late twentieth century
n our opinion, do well to take account. These areas of concern frequently
as it happens.

to our method: since, broadly speaking, the first crucial issue Mackintosh
is the ecclesiastical one; since he then concentrated on philosophy and the-
d since, finally, he worked in the heartland of theology, there follow, in
apters on "The Church and the Means of Grace," "Philosophy and Theism,"
eology and Ethics."

PART TWO: THE THOUGHT
―――――――――――――

CHAPTER III

THE CHURCH AND THE MEANS OF GRACE

Dr. Mackintosh was a churchman. The fact requires fairly forceful state
as a check both upon those who might be tempted to see him as one who "freel
his way through life, sitting lightly to creeds, confessions and all things eccle
cally corporate; and upon any latter day Congregationalists who might be led
pose that Mackintosh's suspicion of undue organisation and bureaucracy in the
Church blinded him to the necessity of a visible churchly presence in the worl

It is undoubtedly true that Mackintosh who, after all, had had more exper
than most of what he regarded as constricted, hidebound, organised religion,
suspicious of any ecclesiastical system which could so entrammel a person's
conscience as to suggest that gospel is subservient to system. In his penultim
book he protested, "we should better realise the moral value of the Christian
Church if we could think of it more as a fellowship and less as an organisatior
But, as his very first book made plain, he regarded the Church as Christ's o\
foundation, and as being implicit in the idea of mission. The Church qua orga
tion was not, however, (and pace some of Mackintosh's contemporaries) the p
mount concern of Christ during his ministry. That position was occupied by tl
concept and fact of the Kingdom, and the terms "Church" and "Kingdom" were
synonymous (125). Later, and in a different connection, Mackintosh urged the
point when, following in the wake of Schleiermacher and Ritschl on the questic
redemption, he said, "Whatever else is true about redemption, the New Testa
compels us to see in it more than an individual blessing; and the constitution
preservation of a church must be recognised as part of the Redeemer's work"
It does not follow, however, that a Christian should violate his own conscienc
vis a particular Christian communion. On the contrary, there may be occasio
when the Christian "must be loyal to his own conscience, and take all risks" (
At the same time, secession should be a last resort, and some people tire of
organised church far too quickly:

> "Doubtless our churches are poor and unworthy representatives of
> their amazingly glorious ideal. They are dull. They are common-
> place. They are even lukewarm. Yet we have reason to trust that
> they are precious in God's sight, for Jesus Christ's sake; and shall
> they not be precious in ours? ... I do not feel able to say to the
> solitary soul which despises Church fellowship, 'You cannot pos-
> sibly follow Christ in isolation.' But this one must say: 'A Christian
> life led in isolation, when it might be led in fellowship, is a Chris-
> tian life mutilated. It neither gets what it might from Church mem-
> bership, nor gives what it ought to the common cause' (128)."

The question arises, what are the terms of association with this fellowshi
have already traced the anguish of Dr. Mackintosh as he worked out his practi

to this question. We have now to consider the theoretical conclusions he
[as to creeds, confessions, and subscription.

I

ring the course of his writing life Robert Mackintosh launched a number of
upon the notion of credal subscription in general, and upon subscription to
itminster Confession of Faith in particular. The conclusions to which he was
at the outset of his ministry were echoed throughout his life, though before
ing these a cautionary word must be uttered. The bald assertion that
:osh was wary of creeds and confessions, and particularly of the Westminster
iion, must not be allowed to obscure his very real grasp upon the essential
hristian faith: trust in Christ as Saviour and Lord. On this he never wavered;
iterest of this he fought. His position may be outlined under three headings:

historical difficulty

re the crux of the matter is that "we are different men from the Westminster
, and have different minds from theirs" (129). It is not that truth changes,
i's grasp of it does, and Mackintosh felt that for at least four reasons men
ay could not rest content with a seventeenth century Confession. In the first
he growth of toleration had dealt the death blow to Puritan strategy in respect
ssional subscription. The Puritans had expected the state to uphold the Con-
- by force if need be. Toleration had rendered this policy impracticable, and
ilting individualistic conception of religion, whilst not without its own dangers,
strong as to rule out any possibility of setting the clock back. Secondly, the
tic activities of the eighteenth century had necessitated that Christians should
riously the arguments and doubts of sceptics, and seek to make a more ra-
esponse than the "vulgar calumny, 'You are a bad man and a hypocrite' "(130).
was the very conclusion to which a straightforward reading of the West-
Confession's teaching on man's inability led one. Thirdly, the Evangelical
, with its warm outreach to those outside the Church challenged that hyper-
stic lethargy in mission which resulted from the belief that Christ was not
world, but only for the elect. As we shall later observe, Mackintosh did not
of the undue stress which many evangelicals placed on conversion, or of the
3 of revivalism; but he did feel that evangelicals had made a great spiritual
(entailing a departure from traditional orthodoxy) in judging doctrines by
actical and experimental significance. Indeed, he went so far as to express
ion that this "architectonic" principle would reconstruct theology within the
y years or decades. Its influence would, he surmised, be felt not least upon
rpretation of the Bible, whose real subject is not inscrutable mysteries but
is experience. Fourthly, the advent of Biblical criticism rendered impossible
l of appeal which had been made to scripture by the framers of the West-
Confession.

э conclusion is that no confession of faith may be exalted into a test of faith
ime. So to be tied to a confession would be to be tied not only to the excel-

lences, but also to the thought forms and to the mistakes of men of former tir
This would be an unenviable position to be in, for thought forms inevitably cha
with the passage of the years, and mistakes are open to correction. The Chri
should neither wish to bolster up archaism nor to perpetuate error.

(b) The content of the Westminster Confession

The Confession presupposes that salvation is confined to Christians only.
Mackintosh this notion was "apologetically valueless, and wholly out of touch
moral ideas" (131). It derived from the confessional emphasis upon law rathe
grace. Calvinism made the mistake of attempting to

> "reason inductively from the facts of providence, inferring sovereigi
> election and sovereign reprobation from the observed course of the
> gospel in human society; whereas we ought rather to carry with us tl
> light of God's revealed character as what illuminates the darkness of
> our experience, and, it may be, transforms our first impressions of
> the ways of Providence by showing us that we had been blind so far to
> more than half the truth" (132).

The effect of Calvinism's mistake is two-fold. In the first place it undermines
we know of God's <u>character</u>. If it be true that God is love, then the gospel wil
with its own light, irrespective of my understanding of anything it will do for
But if God's will for the salvation of sinners is revealed as an arbitrary unex
fact then the only subjective motive for believing it is a desire to escape from
consequences of sin (133). He wishes to maintain that

> "Christian faith is primarily faith in the character of God as love,
> and as therefore naturally, though in marvellous grace, interposing
> to save His children. Calvinism knows nothing of God's character,
> except that He is an inflexible lawgiver. The revealed character of
> God is represented as condemning the sinner; our hopes are built
> not on the Divine character, but on the arbitrary or inscrutable will
> of God" (134).

The point is underlined elsewhere: "For the theology of early Israel, as for H
Calvinism and probably for many of the Moslem schools, God would cease to I
vine if He might not indulge in the fullest caprice" (135). Calvinism, as repre
by no less a person than Dr. Hodge, is quite happy to contemplate God's blanc
activity in respect of the unsaved. Against Hodge Mackintosh protests:

> "when I find that God Almighty, the most righteous and loving, make
> a free offer of salvation, I assume that it is genuinely free and <u>bona
> fide</u>, not merely in the Calvinistic sense - for the <u>bona fide</u> offer of
> salvation by a Calvinistic God is quite compatible with a fixed resolu
> tion to destroy you eternally - but in the straightforward and simple
> sense of the words. Who is Dr. Hodge, that he should act as guardiai
> of the Divine dignity? Is he in sympathy with the God whom he affects
> to represent" (136)?

y, and by implication, Calvinism undermines the genuinely Christian under-
₃ of faith as personal trust. On a strictly substitutionary line, faith would
be understood as a person's <u>assent</u> to the arrangement God has made on his
But such a view seems to evacuate faith of most of its religious meaning (137).
inism proceeds to assert that we <u>cannot</u> thus assent without the aid of the
irit. In other words, we are morally dependent on God after all. "Morality
l at the eleventh hour; and the doctrine of inability, which at first sight
d merely odious, turns out to be a link by which the theology of substitution
ected with the postulates of moral life" (138). Mackintosh's rueful conclusion
'the only mystery about Calvinism is, that men should ever have received it
uthentic doctrine of the God and Father of our Saviour Jesus Christ" (139).

issue of subscription

Mackintosh fully appreciated the motives which had led his forebears to
confessional subscription. With the coming of toleration and the resulting inism in religion, it was necessary that at least the ministers, that is, those
with speaking officially in the Church's name, should not teach contrary to
rch's generally received doctrines. "Their only serious error was in the
nd scholastic character of the creed they imposed; and that error was the
their age" (140). The result of subscription, however, was that an hierarchi-
ge was driven between the clergy and the laity, so that "the broad general
f the present system is, that the Christian people are men of the Bible, and
isters men of the Westminster Confession" (141). As if this were not enough,
osh was confronted by two further problems: how could he both maintain
tual integrity and assent to "truth claims" concerning the falsity of which he
10 doubt? And, above all, how could he reconcile his conscience, consequent
oscribing to a Confession concerning whose morality he had the gravest re-
ons? The Church must never forget that she is a learner; and free discussion
dispensable condition of a growing knowledge of the truth. "But, if this is to
in mind, there must be no pledging of Church teachers to stale scholastic
es in regard to non-essentials" (142).

revert to the point we made at the outset: despite Mackintosh's grave reser-
concerning subscription, the evangelical experience of God's grace in Christ
him absolutely fundamental. Hence, if pressed on the question of an indis-
e minimum of belief, he would first point out that, confronted by such a love
s our best explanations are grossly inadequate, and then continue:

> "By implication, a very narrow circle of known truths, a very dim
> apprehension of their grounds and of their force, suffices to bring an
> empty soul into relation to all the fulness of God. That is true faith,
> in its extreme weakness, but also in its inestimable preciousness.
> Such "implication" of belief is a very different thing from mechanically
> saying "ditto" to the Church and to the hierarchy" (143).

s the end of his life Mackintosh expressed the point more specifically, thus:

> "One feature is uniform in all the Christologies of the <u>N.T.</u> - within

43

the Gospels, I am convinced as much as within the Epistles - all of
them call Jesus 'Lord.' That confession of faith, I believe, is the
minimum Christology upon which the Christian Church ever can live.
Perhaps the <u>maximum</u> Christological creed, which is suitable for
educated modern Christian minds, will not differ much from this minimum" (144).

Though he found much to complain of in the Westminster Confession, and
withstanding his refusal to approve the practice of credal or confessional subs
Mackintosh had no quarrel with the composition of confessions designed to wit
to the faith commonly held by those in whose name they were drafted (145). E⋅
Westminster Confession could be used as "a symbol of continuity of religious
and a pledge, that we wish to build on the old foundations..." (146). Indeed, i
hoves Christians to be on their guard

> "against Unitarian critics who assume that in every Church a creed
> carries finality with it, and that those who would be free must be cre
> less. Neither of a man nor of a Church is that true. We are not witho
> law to God; we are under law to Christ. Creeds may be, and if they
> exist at all ought to be, accepted as a progressive apprehension of
> Christian truth" (147).

II

By the time he wrote the words just quoted Dr. Mackintosh had been settl
his new spiritual home, Congregationalism, for some seventeen years. We ha
ready seen that he regarded himself as a refugee from Free Church confessio
and found in Congregationalism a congenial home. In his address to the Intern
Congregational Council (1920) on "The Contribution of British Congregationali
Religious Thought: our Present Strength and Weakness in that Field," he side(
the Commission on which he had served in applauding the fact that the Congre
tionalism of his day was more, not less, loyal to the genius of that order. In
of this he cited the fact that state churchism, a binding creed, the doctrine of
plenary inspiration of the scriptures, and the hard substitutionary theory of th
atonement, had all been discarded. He rejoiced to think that "it is an immens(
valuable option for the Christian mind, or for the mind striving to be Christia
it may still follow the Congregational plan and be loyal to the uttermost towar(
Son of David, without finding it necessary to wear the armour of King Saul" (1
Grave disservice would be done to Dr. Mackintosh, however, if such a passag
not balanced by the one previously quoted, or by such a comment as this: "I p(
ly might be willing to see a new statement of faith drawn up, and even to toler
express acceptance of such a statement by our ministers - an acceptance in g(
terms, not a vow of detailed loyalty to its several theses" (149). As he himsel
he was no free-lance; and the Congregationalism he entered had not been afra
declare those things commonly held by its members in the Savoy Declaration (
and the Declaration of Faith adopted in 1833 following the formation of the Cor

...ion of England and Wales (150). We may perhaps summarise what was the
...cially favourable feature of Congregationalism in Mackintosh's eyes by saying
...in that fellowship a Christian may cleave unreservedly to Christ as Saviour
..., and yet be left to walk by faith rather than by sight in many matters of
... practice.

... significant that Dr. Mackintosh's explicit accounts of his coming to Congre-
...ism are exclusively in terms of his spiritual difficulties with the Church of
...rs. He nowhere says that he came to Congregationalism because he felt that
...munion was saying something important and distinctive concerning the nature
...urch. Unlike some other converts to that fold, Mackintosh stood in primary
... conscience at peace rather than of a more amenable theology of the Church.
...r, since he came to believe that "Christianity as a polity, when trimmed of
...ous fat and reduced to its innermost essence, is Congregationalism" (151),
... use the terms "Christianity" and "Congregationalism" virtually synonymous -
...without stressing distinctive political features.

...ards the end of his life Mackintosh was invited to contribute a paper on "The
...f Congregationalism" to Essays Congregational and Catholic. Here his con-
...very much the positive one of stressing Congregationalism's understanding
...hurch as being a fellowship whose being and continuity depend "under God,
... creeds or councils or hierarchies but upon the fact that the friends of
...re able to recognize one another at sight" (152). Not indeed that the Church
... of any collection of individuals. It is not the case that "the floating mass of
...isible visitors is to bear rule in the house of God ... the church and not the
...ation must accept the burden of responsibility and excercise the rights of
... freemen" (153). To Mackintosh all of this is clear beyond question:

"The local church, when necessity requires or expediency counsels,
can function - without reference to Christians elsewhere - as the
Church of Christ, with Christ's fullest blessing resting upon it....
The Christian church consists of Christians - of those who share the
new life. It is not merely, it is not necessarily, experience of a
crisis of conversion that makes the difference between Christian and
non-Christian; but the difference is infinite.
>   The Church's one foundation
>   Is Jesus Christ her Lord;
>   She is His new creation.
That is the eternal truth, to which Congregationalism bears an eternal
witness. If we lose that, we forfeit everything" (154).

...arks just quoted appear in a context of objection to any quadrilateral - Lam-
...other. There is but one foundation - Christ. No one may exalt other principles
...it of equality with him, and no one may wrest the Christian freeman's privi-
...d responsibilities from him. Because of his stress upon these latter, we are
...rised to note that Mackintosh viewed with a certain amount of suspicion the
... towards centralisation in Congregationalism. In the course of a discussion
...-collegiate co-operation in Manchester he refers to the harm that could be
..."those extremists of New School Congregationalism who would regulate

everything from a central office" (155). At the same time he welcomed the in[troduction] of the moderatorial system according to which the nine provinces of England [and] Wales enjoyed the care of a <u>pastor pastorum</u>, "provided there is no nonsense [of] apostolical succession ... provided further there is no smallest mimicry of t[he] real Anglican vow of canonical obedience to a bishop" (156).

We may conclude that Dr. Mackintosh found in Congregationalism good C[hristian] fellowship, a lack of intellectual and moral constraint, a worthy desire to co[nfer] responsibility to every member, and a fit organ of mission. Above all, the c[harac-] <u>teristic</u> stance of Congregationalism was, he felt, avowedly evangelical:

> " 'Democratic' control of policy, within the Church, may be the shell
> of Congregationalism but never its kernel. The body of Congregatio-
> nalism might continue to exist for a season, though it had ceased to [be]
> an expression of evangelical faith and life; but the soul which has ani-
> mated it would be gone. And a body without its soul is a corpse" (157[).

III

In his very first book Robert Mackintosh advanced the view that "Scriptur[e, as] understood by those who are Christ's, and who, therefore, normally and prop[erly] constitute the Church ..." (158). What, then, was his understanding of the na[ture] and function of the book of the people of God?

To a quite remarkable degree we find premonitions of later biblical theol[ogy in] Mackintosh. This is tantamount to saying that he steered a middle course bet[ween] those who would idolise the Book, and those who would cause it to disintegrat[e under] critical fire. Thus on the one hand we find that he rounds upon those who will [not] admit that the Bible contains any errors of fact or of moral judgement. On th[is] question he cheerfully accepts many of the findings of biblical criticism: "the[re may] be doctrinal divergences in Scripture; there may be scientific errors; there [may be] historical discrepancies. Yet, if Scripture brings us into contact with God an[d] Christ, it does its work. Its work, no doubt, implies the presence of the Holy [Spirit.] But what the Holy Spirit attests is the general scheme of the Gospel, under w[hich] Christ lays hold of men's hearts - not any intellectual calculation" (159). Els[ewhere] he distinguishes between revelation and inspiration. The locus of revelation i[s histo-] rical, in Israel-Christ. Scripture is a first reflection of revealed facts. "Hen[ce] saving faith in Christ is a faith in God's revelations and deeds of redemption. [Our] saving faith does not necessarily imply the infallibility of the lost autographs [of the] Bible, any more than the infallibility of the Codex Alexandrinus or of King Ja[mes] version" (160).

On the other hand, Mackintosh did not concede everything to the critics. [As far] as he was concerned, "criticism deals only with probabilities, - a fact, whicl [one] wishes the critics would themselves bear in mind" (161). It is a tribute to his [sense] of balance as well as to his intellectual integrity that Mackintosh, who had liv[ed] through the Robertson Smith episode, and felt the full force of the new criticis[m,] should resolutely have refused to clamber aboard either of the opposing band[s.]

ay. Though unsensational, he was as we have suggested, quietly prophetic.
ll become clear if, having noted the Scylla and Charybdis he avoided, we
rise his positive position.

r Mackintosh the Bible is "man's book, written, and needing to be read, in
ght, with the help of God's Spirit ..." (162). It is, as certain later biblical
ans have never ceased to remind us, the book of promise and of fulfilment;
focal point is Christ. "The New Testament history, or the New Testament
.re a substantial fulfilment of Old Testament aspirations - partly in that they
perfectly to mankind what the Old Testament could only imperfectly con-
irtly, too, because they fulfil (in their own way) the hopes which the Old
ent had awakened in the breasts of God's people" (163). But our understand-
ie Bible is gravely impaired unless we bring it in relation to the high peak
ation - Christ himself:

> "That is what is distinctive in the Bible, - it is the only original source
> for the knowledge of God in Christ. Christ is the revelation: the Bible
> is the medium by which the revelation reaches us. All other merits that
> we may claim, however justly, on behalf of the Bible, are only prole-
> gomena to its real claim, - that it enshrines God's last message, God's
> highest gift. Let us get face to face with Christ in our apologetic.
> Faith in Him saves a man. And the moral conviction that God is in
> Christ gives the one true spiritual certainty - the witness of the Spi-
> rit - to the gospel message. This certainty does not attach to details.
> We cannot make our moral emotions guarantee the details, either of
> the text of Scripture, or of the narrative" (164).

fter criticism has done its work we are left with an inescapable challenge -
)nd, or not. Here we are thrown upon our own resources, and are required
1 the moral probability of the alternatives. "And in that region the humblest
ned with sincerity and purity is as wise as the most learned" (165).

IV

at of the Church's sacraments ? We shall be aided in our understanding of
:osh's position here if we keep firmly in mind the distinction he draws between
entalism and sacramentarianism; if we remember that he had lived through
od of the Anglo-Catholic revival in the Church of England - a period which
me present-day "advanced" Anglicans would brand "the Victorian-medieval"
e note that, without argument, he limits his treatment of the sacraments to
baptism and the Lord's supper, pausing only to remark of the Council of
hich claimed as <u>de fide</u> five further dominically instituted sacraments, that
logy that will say that will say anything" (166).

. Mackintosh argues that the religious essence of Catholicism is sacramental

> "Here, in the sacrament ... the High Churchman finds the grace of

God. He knows, like all other Christians, that he cannot save himsel[f]
he knows that God saves him in ways that go beyond his knowledge; h[e]
believes that God saves him through the sacred rites of the Church.
Deny him these, or deny the meaning that he puts upon them, and the
High Churchman is tempted to cry out, "Ye have taken away my
gods" "(167).

For his part, Mackintosh does not deny that normally God's grace works thro[ugh]
sacramental - and other - means. But he objects to the exaltation of one form
the type or explanation of grace. Thus he can say, "The sacraments are a wit[ness to]
God's grace - a channel for God's grace - everything the high churchman can [claim for]
them, except a substitute for God's grace, or a shackle upon God's free Spiri[t".]
If we piece together his scattered utterances on the theme we find him aware [of]
dangers in particular which attach to sacramentarianism. Firstly, it can lead [to]
superstition. "If wicked men keep on terms of bare civility with the Church, a[nd]
resort to her for an occasional whitewashing, she is bound to promise them s[alva]-
tion - in the lowest degree, perhaps, but still salvation" (169). If any of his co[n-]
temporaries should protest that this comment were justified only in face of an [ex-]
treme and nowadays untypical sacramentarianism, Mackintosh could quote an [un-]
named) Anglo-Catholic writer who defined the sacramental principle as "the b[asis of]
the transmission of spiritual power by material means". For Mackintosh, "Su[rely]
the definition is enough to condemn the doctrine" (170). Secondly, when associ[ated]
with what Mackintosh held to be an erroneous doctrine of the episcopate, sacr[amen-]
tarianism bred exclusiveness and schism within the body of Christ. It is not t[hat he]
objected to the very word "episcopacy". On the contrary, he could see that de[spite]
its lack of divine, apostolic, demonstrable credentials, the episcopate could, [as]
part of a wider system of government, greatly benefit God's cause (171). But
linked with sacramentarianism, one must protest that "Christianity cannot be [both]
the finished revelation of moral and spiritual truth, and also a system of supe[r-]
magic" (172). Paul's support is invoked at this point:

> "Useless practices, personal eccentricities, he regarded with a larg[e]
> and easy tolerance; he contented himself with labelling rudimentary
> ritualists as "the weak." But when this weakness met him as an
> organised theory, an aggressive superstition, unchurching all who di[d]
> not share its practices, then he cut at its very roots by forbidding the
> practices in question. Why? It had exchanged the gospel for another
> private gospel "which was not another" "(173).

Thirdly, sacramentarianism can bring about the erosion of the genuinely Chri[stian]
distinctives. This was one of the charges Mackintosh levelled against the Rep[ort of]
the 1925 COPEC Conference. An attempt is made in the Report (174) to argue [that]
the natural world is sacramental in that it is replete with spiritual meanings.
Mackintosh, however, "The discovery of ideal beauty in the world is too weak [an]
argument to efface the reiterated impression of nature's indifference, still m[ore]
disprove nature's apparent cruelty" (175). This point is made in the interest o[f]
as constituting the best indication that nature is not unconcerned with moral th[ings.]
Perhaps Mackintosh reads too much into the Report at this point. The Christi[an can]
surely hold both that his God may address him through the beauties and ambig[uities]

e, and also that man is our best created clue to the reality of the moral.
ly the COPEC Report does not pretend to find a solution to the problem of
the mere contemplation of natural beauty. Again, Mackintosh holds,

> "A grave issue is raised when we are told (176) that revelation is
> "given through the medium (1) of the material," and only "(2) of
> the personal." ... I am inclined to submit that God's action, whether
> in revelation or in grace, is personal "first, second, and all the time,"
> and that the opposite view would legitimate gross belief in magic" (177).

s conclusion we may heartily concur. What is doubtful is whether the COPEC
rs would dispute it. Even if they have the order wrong, do they not intend
s the personal God who reveals himself through his creation - He and no
od? Be all this as it may, we can readily see why Mackintosh, after a dis-
of Augustine's view of the sacraments, welcomes the emphasis upon the
ents as "directly embodying God's good will and His purpose to save," but
und to add the expostulation, "Yet how treacherous an embodiment they
.78). Nor are we surprised to discover that Dr. Mackintosh's answer to the
i, "Are the sacraments a sine qua non of salvation?" is a resounding nega-
the context of a discussion of Moberly's atonement theology which would, by
ss upon the need for continuous sacramental participation "rob us of what our
termed 'the finished work of Christ'" he asserts that "the sacraments can
distinctive part in theology or in the Christian revelation" (179). This is not
l to imply any depreciation of the sacraments - and Mackintosh grants the
ity that they have been depreciated within Protestantism. But still, as he
re says, "With or without sacramental vehicles, faith blesses, enriches,
es the soul of the Christian man" (180). He underlined this view even more
lly in a letter to the editor of the Manchester Guardian written on 31st
, 1927:

> "Jesus Christ, who was so many greater things, was also a poet, and
> spoke as a poet when he said "This is my body." Crass literalism and
> dogged dogmatism have turned our Poet into a thaumaturgist. Even
> Anglicanism seems to tolerate any extravagance of materialistic super-
> stition so long as the word "Transubstantiation" is avoided. There is a
> "spiritual" presence, says the High Anglican tradition, of Jesus Christ's
> "body". This formula is presented to us as a holy mystery; those of us
> who are not Anglicans incline to regard it and similar "mysterious"
> doctrines as in the strictest sense meaningless. Wrong is done by such
> sacramentalism, not merely to common sense or to science, or even
> to intellectual honesty, but to the central evangelical thesis - that we
> are saved, not by swallowing consecrated communion elements, but by
> the infinite mercy of God our Father, revealed to us and bestowed upon
> us in Jesus Christ."

inal general comment is in order before we proceed to consider Dr. Mackin-
nderstanding of the two dominical sacraments. Lest it should appear that his
es were directed entirely against the Catholic wing of the Church, it should
l that he had stern things to say against that form of Puritanism which, as

far as the sacraments were concerned, so paved the way to the Lord's Table
self-examination, humiliation and fasting, that the sacrament, "instead of bei
the centre of Christian fellowship, as in the early Church, was to be a rare a
ceptional privilege" (181). The effect of this was that "Doctrinally and emotio
(the believer) was to live by grace; but his conduct was to be exactly the sam(
he expected to be justified by law" (182). None of which, we need hardly add,
all to Dr. Mackintosh's liking.

It is no part of our purpose to discuss Mackintosh's account of the biblica
dence concerning either Baptism or the Lord's Supper (183). Suffice it to say
felt a much stronger case could be made in favour of Christ's institution of th
than of the former, but that "a certain element of doubt exists whether Jesus
literally founded either of the two New Testament sacraments" (184). By Paul
however, it had become clear (see I Cor. x) that room had to be found for the
ordinances whose spiritual significance was so great (185).

Mackintosh's understanding of the significance of Baptism emerges clear
the course of a discussion of revivalism. He holds that both the High Churchn
and the ranting revivalist are individualists, for the former's community is "
aggregate of baptized individuals," the latter's, "of converted" individuals (1{
But "to suppose that sprinkling water on an unconscious baby brings it within
charmed circle of God's gracious influences is certainly not a more moral op
than the view that a conscious paroxysm of conversion brings the soul within t
charmed circle" (187). More positively, he claims that "infant baptism is cer
a means of good in admonishing parents, children, and the community, of the
of duty and grace. It stands as the one bulwark against the destruction of the (
in favour of the evangelistic committee" (188).

Yet Mackintosh did not feel entirely at ease with Baptism. In his Christia
Ethics he wrote, "Infant baptism, however seemly in itself, ought not to be ca
a sacrament" (189), and this view he reaffirmed when addressing the Internat
Congregational Council in 1920 (190). His ground was that Baptism seemed m
more clearly an event in the life of the parents than in that of the child. He co
see more point in baptism on the mission field, where the rite would symboli;
though not create, the convert's sense of peace with God through Christ (191)
here at home the rite was surrounded by pitfalls. By the free admission to ba]
of the children of all comers we "make ourselves accomplices in producing a
superstitious impression connected with the outward rite" (192). One mitigatii
tor was that although parents often failed in their post-baptismal duties, Cong
tionalists at least were "free of the system of sponsors - a masterpiece of re
unreality" (193).

What one misses here is a sufficiently clear affirmation of Baptism's sta1
a sacrament of the Church. The role of the gathered, covenanted, fellowship
mentioned, and whilst we know only too well that the upholding of theory does
ways quell mismanagement in practice, it does seem that only by according d
to the notion of the covenanted people of God and to the baptised child's place
that fellowship, can those superstitions which Mackintosh rightly feared be ta

even in his address to the International Congregational Council on the
nts does Mackintosh deal fully with the meaning of the Lord's Supper. Once
e has to piece together relevant material culled from a number of sources
to present a more or less rounded picture. Certainly he was no mere
alist:

> "Every time we break the bread and share the cup, it is as though
> God himself were saying to us - Christ is more needful to you than
> food, or light, or air; Christ is utterly sufficient to cleanse and to
> bless you; Christ who is all this, waits upon you now ... " (194).

hardly add that Mackintosh does not attempt to say how Christ is present,
does he localise him in the elements. The spiritual state of the recipient
tant. Whilst our faith does not conjure up Christ, nevertheless he only comes who exercises faith in God through Christ (195). This is what saves - not
the ordinance per se.

> "Accordingly, what as Protestant evanglicals we Congregationalists
> stand for is the two-fold assertion - the Christian sacrament is truly
> a means of grace; but the sacrament bestows nothing which is not
> accessible to simple faith - which is not pledged, and granted, to
> Christian prayer. ... Sacramental grace - yes; special sacramental
> grace - no; ... for the assertion of a special grace peculiar to sacra-
> ments means the denial of the spirituality of the Christian salvation
> and of the sufficiency of the gospel of the Lord Jesus. So we appear
> to stand midway between those who would suppress or belittle the
> sacraments and those who would attach to them an excessive and un-
> worthy significance. We have to fight a battle on two fronts" (196).

udes that though the sacraments are not vital to Christianity, the two spiritual
or which they stand are. These values are grace and fellowship. Concerning
er, "the sacrament is an ever-renewed witness that God has given to us
ife, and that this life is in His Son" (197); and as to the latter, "While sacra-
eligion ... stands for the recognized preciousness of the individual persona-
cannot come in with the mob; he must have his own individual share in the
e; it stands also for the significance of the fellowship, i.e. with us, of the
in whose gatherings each personality meets with the Real Presence of God
hrist" (198). Hence, despite the dangers to which they may tend, and the
es which surround them, Mackintosh would never dispense with the sacra-
'If we can, we ought rather to claim the Christian sacraments for Christ,
them, and reverently to employ them in his service" (199).

ally, who may preside at the Table? Dr. Mackintosh, though recognising
tailed a breaking with the letter of earlier Congregationalism (200), wel-
le growth among Congregationalists of his day of the view that a non-
ial Church member may serve in this capacity. Indeed, "The Assembly
me for the autumn of 1931, which proposes to carry this principle into
, is a memorable historical landmark" (201). Such a practice, he elsewhere
does not disparage the ministry, but rather testifies to "our reverence for
bership when it is what it ought to be" (202). Implicitly here is the notion of

51

the priesthood of all believers; the idea that the minister is himself a church whose difference from his fellow members is one of normal function and not o and an assertion of the right of the local church to invite whom it will to serve president at what is after all the Lord's table.

In more recent times there has been a return to the earlier view, and Ma tosh himself prophesied that this might happen, especially if union with Metho and Presbyterians were to come about. The custom he favoured might then be lished as "a dangerous irregularity" (203).

A fundamental question concerning doctrinal development is here raised. gregationalists came to accept the ordination of women in theory and in practi They came to accept lay presidency at the Lord's Table. There appears to ha been no going back with respect to the former, but a tightening with respect tc latter. There would seem to be a case for a fresh examination of the question, the possibility that not all 'developments' are in accordance with the will of Gc what are the criteria for determining which are, and which are not?"

V

We conclude this chapter with a brief review of Mackintosh's ideas on the of the Church; on the relation of the Church to the state; and on the relation o Christianity to other religions.

Robert Mackintosh lived through the early, pioneering days of the modern ecumenical movement. He was an active supporter of the Student Christian Mc ment, and in his written statements on things ecumenical he displayed that bal caution to which we have already become accustomed. In the first place, he m tains that there exists already a genuine catholicity, and he roundly declares t Congregationalists share it. It consists in fidelity to the elemental truths of th gospel. He has no patience with the "Anglican fancy" that Congregationalists u church themselves, indeed, he brands it a "schismatic prejudice" (204). As tc nature and source of Christian unity, his comment on I Corinthians i.10 is ins tive:

> "The Church was a unity, but party spirit, the real spirit of evil schism, raged. Separation of denomination from denomination, even if not desirable in itself, need not mean "schism." Union of jealous competing congregations in one organisation is no remedy. But how is such unity possible as Paul demands? Many men, many minds! True, but, abiding in Christ we shall have all essential spiritual oneness in Him" (205).

It would be a mistake to read this as merely a justification of the "painless" u which denies the scandal of a divided Table, and so on, and is so greatly disaj of by the keenly ecumenical. On the contrary, as to visible union Mackintosh s "Where union is legitimate and is practicable, disunion can hardly be anything than sin" (206); and he was not at all averse to exploring whatever possibilitie

ight be of uniting with the English Prebyterians and Baptists (207). At the
ne, he feared any union which would play into the hands of the sacramenta-
8), or which would draw Congregationalism into a more elaborately eccle-
l and credal polity (209). He even maintained, somewhat sardonically, that
of the advantages of disunity were not to be sniffed at:

"as far as we can see, nothing else would have brought toleration into
the world except the circumstance that no one body of Christians in a
country was strong enough to hang and oppress other Christians ...
Is there any nation so badly governed at present that it might not be
far worse misgoverned under the iron sceptre of an oecumenical
priesthood" (210)?

we might expect, Dr. Mackintosh was especially critical of some of the ideas
ling the concept of "the historic episcopate" - that Anglican treasure whose
vere, in his day, being warmly commended to nonconformists. He could not
nd how it came about that an Anglican could, at one and the same time,
it to hold the High Church doctrine that episcopacy were the esse of the
and yet refuse even to contemplate surrendering it:

"They will never give it up. - Not even if it were God's will that they
should? Not even for the love of Christ? Oh, but - they say - the thing
is inconceivable. Why? If episcopacy exists by Divine right, it is
doubtless inconceivable that God should abolish it. But was not that
precisely the assertion which it was intended to avoid? ... To treat
things which are not admittedly essential as if they were essential is
to pass under the Caudine Forks; it is an act of surrender" (211).

er maintained that the earliest form of episcopacy was by way of being an
cy measure designed to provide the war-cry: "Hold to the bishop that you may
d of Christ;" and that its character resembled much more closely that of the
ational pastoral office than that of the modern diocesan episcopate (212). The
difficulty, however, was that episcopal theory was inextricably interwoven
ramental:

"There are two distinct views of Christianity. According to one, salvation is radically sacramental; to express the thing clearly, if uncivil-
ly, is magical. According to the other, salvation is essentially moral;
it comes by faith in God through Christ. The difference is not reduced
to unity by the fact that sacramentalists and evangelicals are included
within the same organisation; it will not disappear even if we Nonconformists are poured into the mixture" (213).

came to advocate a provisional federation with the Anglican Church, based
principle,

"Whom Christ receives, Christians must receive; whom Christ
excludes, Christians ought to repel - that is rudimentary Congregationalism because it is rudimentary Christianity. ... The trouble is
that High churchmanship cannot feel sure Christ receives anyone who
is not sealed with the Episcopal Church's approval. The trouble is,

> that many High churchmen do not regard us as fellow Christians but
> rather as catechumens, who by the proper processes of disinfecting
> may turn into real episcopalian Christians at last. I cannot see that
> we ought to encourage such an attitude. It would be paltry to oppose i
> if it were merely harsh towards us; but there is much more behind.
> We are entrusted with the Gospel. Our duty is to maintain our witnes
> before every man's conscience that -
> The Church's one foundation
> Is Jesus Christ her Lord" (214).

Finally, if ever union with an episcopal church were to be tolerated, the episc in question would have to be a reformed one, and not just the "historic" one:

> "If one ever were to submit to so questionable a process as re-ordi-
> nation, I think one had rather be re-ordained by Moravian than by
> Anglican bishops - by representatives of a free and evangelical churc
> rather than by dignitaries who are certainly not the one and possibly
> not the other. Yet perhaps it might be safer and more really Christia
> to rest content with the ordination we have - by the call of a Congreg;
> tional church, and, as we trust, by the blessing of God" (215).

Dr. Mackintosh's views on the relation of Church and state must be read a the background of his own spiritual pilgrimage. He had been reared in a Churc mitted to the establishment principle, though it was not, in fact, the establish Church. Even if it be true that, as Dr. Laughton, a Disruption minister, once to Mackintosh, the Disruption fathers' disenchantment with the Established Ch caused them to minimise the importance of the establishment principle, it is (the case that the issue came to the fore as union with the voluntarist United P terian Church drew near (216). In this latter context Robert Mackintosh wrest the problem.

He boldly claims that through the National Covenant and (after the union o Crowns) the Solemn League and Covenant, the Scottish Church was pledged "tc nal loyalty towards the threefold ideal - Calvinism, Presbyterianism, intolera (217). But when this position became entangled with the classical Puritan insis upon the concept of Christ's Church as a _spiritual_ body, contradiction resultec Hence, in one paragraph the Westminster Confession urges that it is the Chur prerogative to determine religious truth and duty, whilst elsewhere the Confes remits this function to the State (218). Mackintosh concludes that the only expl of the failure of the agile minds which drafted the Confession to see the contra was their intolerant habit of thought. They could not entertain as a possibility notion that sincere minds might differ with them over the nature of truth (219) Hence "the ideals of Scottish Church life never fully adjusted themselves to th principle of toleration" (220).

Mackintosh saw that the growth of toleration, leading to the widespread ac tance of the belief in the liberty of conscience, tended inevitably to the conclus that the real religious organ of religious duty is the Church, not the state. It i even necessary that the state recognise the Church, and it may even be that th Church establishment principle infringes the _state's_ conscience by asking it to

cheque to the Church (221). He could easily conceive of circumstances in
might be right for the state to offer redress against a pursecuting ecclesiastiority (222). Certainly "in the days of intolerance ... the State was sinning, and
rch was conniving at sin - nay, more, was hounding on the rulers to acts of
3). Happily this was so no longer, and "to unlearn one huge and pernicious
is to travel by a whole continent nearer the land which we desire" (224).

times Mackintosh chides the English Establishment. One day the Church of
will reach manhood, and will cease to be carried around by Privy Councils
like! The basic trouble is, he thinks, that Englishmen cannot see that "the
s abandonment of her liberty is <u>pro tanto</u> disloyalty to the will of Christ. ...
res more logical coherence than Providence has allotted to their mental
·e" (225). Again, England "is a nation that dislikes the pain of thinking. It
s ideas. From the judicious Hooker downwards, English theories about
and State are attempts to justify pre-existing and tolerably anomalous facts.
land has indeed a recognised faculty for 'muddling through somehow' "(226).
Mackintosh's objections to establishment was the consideration that a duty
lish necessarily legitimates a duty to pursecute; and the fact that so often
establishment has resulted in control of the Church by the state (227). How-
Disestablishment may come any day; that would interrupt the paralysis of
life, although it is true enough that nothing else is likely to interrupt it" (228).
should not conclude that Mackintosh was an out and out voluntarist:

> "The acceptance of liberty of conscience destroys the older positive
> arguments in favour of an Established Church. And the insistence
> upon spiritual independence renders a satisfactory Establishment
> practically hopeless in modern times. But neither position coincides
> with the pure voluntary doctrine, Every Established Church is unjust" (229).

isidering that Dr. Mackintosh's written contributions cover so wide a field
cal studies, philosophy, ethics, and theology - to say nothing of papers on
neral subjects - it would be churlish to complain that he did not write much
eld of comparative religion. This by no means indicates a lack of interest in
ect on his part: he did in fact teach the subject at Manchester University for
and certainly he could hardly have failed to think through the implications of
ory of religions movement which was developing so rapidly at precisely the
nchester's Faculty of Theology was being mooted. The fact remains that
evidence is scanty, and what little there is is prompted very much by evange-
isiderations. Thus, for example, Hegel is faulted because in terms of his
h "there can be no absolute division, in regard either to origin or quality,
the other faiths of mankind and that faith which dominates the modern world.
stulate of Hegel's is repugnant to ordinary Christian thinking" (230). The
a approach is most attractively stated, according to Mackintosh, by Dr.
ird in his <u>Introduction to the Philosophy of Religion</u>. Caird here allows that
inity is the highest, evolved, religion. But still a qualification is required,
Mackintosh points out, for Christianity the world's religious history is by
is a normal evolution, but is distorted by sin. And this distortion has been

tackled in history by Christ, so that any Hegelian strain which exalts the Chri
while minimising the importance of the historical, is unacceptable (231).

Nor is the distinction between Christianity and other religions merely the
cal: it is practical too:

> "Humble trust in a God, clearly known or dimly felt to be highest
> righteousness and perfect love, may be Christian wherever it
> occurs - may indeed be regarded as the vital heart of Christianity.
> But when we bring the other faiths of mankind into comparison with t
> religion of the Bible (Old Testament or New), how little of trust do w
> find, and how very little of humble trust! Whatever sporadic working
> of the Spirit of redemption may elsewhere appear, the Saviour of the
> world is the creator for the world of those streams of living water -
> humility, penitence, faith in God" (232).

As regards what he called the "sceptical Half-Christianities," Mackintosh wa
fectly prepared for co-operation between them and the Church in the interest
social advance. Nevertheless he avers as a matter of fact, and not in a patror
manner, "Let it be understood that Christians look on their allies as imperfec
enlightened men;" and he hoped that Christians would so assiduously be about
business "that half-Christians may ripen in great numbers into whole-hearted
Christians" (233).

CHAPTER IV

PHILOSOPHY AND THEISM

his chapter and the next we shall be concerned to outline Dr. Mackintosh's
approach to some of the fundamental questions within philosophy and theology.
ount will be necessarily selective, partly because there is little point in re-
in detail Mackintosh's expositions of the thought of those with whom he deals;
tly because some of the issues with which he deals are no longer live. Thus,
nple, we shall refrain from resurrecting in this chapter his discussion of
)bbe's attack upon Darwin's theory of the rise of morals (234); and in the
ipter, the points at which he faulted Dr. A.E. Garvie in respect of some
e of Ritschlian criticism (235). Instead, we shall observe his stance towards
the schools of thought and available options which he passed in review.

I

h its apparently straightforward appeal to facts, and its regard for the
ies of everyday experience, empiricism seemed to Mackintosh to offer the
it basis for philosophy (236). Its exponents could verge upon materialism in
ataphysics, whilst happily embracing determinism in ethics - as had hap-
ι the case of Thomas Hobbes. Not all empiricists were as single-minded,
·. Although John Locke was "the real father of English philosophy" (237) in
called in question the notion of innate ideas as propounded by Descartes and
:rbert of Cherbury, he was "a double-minded or half hearted philosopher.
its two sources of knowledge - sensation and <u>reflexion</u>" (238). Hence he can
d a form of the cosmological argument for God's existence - but such an
it ought to accompany an intuitionalist rather than an empiricist doctrine
ility. Again, whereas in the little Locke says on ethics he is determinist
when he turns to political thought he makes an appeal to natural law. But
further intuitionist, if not idealist, concept. Berkeley sought to modify
materialistic tendencies by introducing the notion of immaterialism, and
ig away from our ideas as testifying to the existence of matter, to God's
ι the subject. But Hume was shortly to point out that, "the inference to God
ecarious as the inference to matter, and that the assertion of a continuous
aterial mind in man also goes beyond the immediate facts" (239). Hence he
it scepticism in English philosophy. Yet Mackintosh questions how far Hume
lly in earnest. He strongly professed his admiration of rational and natural
. "It was not yet socially safe to be a confessed religious sceptic" (240).

shall refer later to Mill's empiricist approach to theism, but meanwhile we
e that one of his objections to the teleological argument was that if evolution-
iry should be clearly established there would be no need to posit a special act
ion - all would have proceeded in accordance with the natural law. Whatever

else may be said of evolution, the word was on the lips of many, from the pro[fes]sional philosopher to the soap box orator, in Mackintosh's early and mid-prof[essional] life. Darwin was by no means the first to remark upon the evolutionary factor [in] living organisms. His originality came to the fore, however, as he sought to [account] for the existence of plants and animals of different species. How had they com[e to be] as they were? His answer was that by a process of natural selection, or what [Spencer] was to call the principle of "the survival of the fittest," our presently existing [species] had struggled for survival, and undergone physical adaptations in accordance [with] the demands which their environment had imposed upon them (241). For his p[art] Spencer was influenced by Grove's proof of the correlation of the physical for[ces] and by Joule's determination of the mechanical equivalent for heat. These adv[ances] prompted his conviction of the organic unity of the physical realm, and togeth[er with] his studies of the new Darwinianism, led him to postulate a physical natural l[aw,] requiring no external causality to assist it, as being the cause of all that is. [His] criterion of the degree of evolution was complexity: the more complex, the m[ore] highly developed the species. Spencer employed two further interpretative cat[egories,] dissolution and equilibration, which Mackintosh defines as follows: "Dissoluti[on is] the opposite of evolution. Equilibration stands between the two - the last stage [of an] evolutionary process within any finite aggregate before the forces of dissoluti[on] break in from the outside" (242). Mackintosh's quarrel with Spencer is that S[pencer] cannot show how, from the formula of "growing complexity" one can deduce o[rgani]sation, consciousness, or history (243).

The most extreme form of empiricism under discussion in Dr. Mackintos[h's] day was positivism, and he treated the thought of Comte in some detail (244). [Comte,] we are told, appeals to facts and rejects the claims of supernatural religion, [meta]physics, introspective psychology and intuition to be cognitive. He traces the [de]velopment of man's theological interpretation of the world from fetishism, thr[ough] polytheism, to monotheism. Parallel sociological developments were concurr[ently] taking place as man became aware of the claims first of family, then of state, [then] of empire. Significantly, Comte does not regard metaphysics as disproved, b[ut] merely as outmoded. He will not be called an atheist, nor yet a materialist. [He is] an agnostic, and, as Mackintosh cheekily expresses it, "He will neither say "[yes]" nor "no." But he is filled with scorn for those who say "yes," for he is perfec[tly] and dogmatically assured that we have no right to dogmatise" (245).

One thinks of certain latter-day positivists at this point. In the interests [of] their attack upon metaphysics they asserted a highly metaphysical theory of v[eri]fication. As Mackintosh says with reference to Comte, "those who despise me[ta]physics far too thoroughly to study it, will always be found rejoicing in scraps [of] metaphysical "creeds outworn" "(246). This emerges <u>inter alia</u> in Comte's ap[peal] to biology. Writing before the rise of evolutionary theory he conceived of soci[ety] on the model of a biological organism. But, complains Mackintosh, it is very [con]venient if, having rejected so many metaphysical authorities, you assert the r[ival] claim of the community and its members. His doctrine of a social organism "[is a] moral dictum, picturesquely stated in terms of popular science" (247). Macki[ntosh's] general conclusion after studying thinkers from Comte to Kidd is that "if biolo[gical] clues are to afford guidance for human conduct, they must be supplemented by

moral and religious light, and in philosophy by some scheme of metaphysical
nism, marking a transition perhaps from "Darwin" to "Hegel" "(248). Dr.
osh, characteristically, tackled no such project. He remained content to
riew which some Christians hold, namely, that "in Jesus Christ, and in Him
re have the pledge of the human world's fulfilling its destiny, of the vanquish-
l the obstacles that can arise, of the great career's reaching, at last, that

> one far-off divine event
> To which the whole creation moves" (249).

re leaving empiricism we should observe that Mackintosh does not take an
essimistic view of the impact of the empirical tendency upon religion. He
is the fact that the strange and varied phenomena of religion are receiving
tention than ever before, and considers that any attention is better than
condly, against that degradation which man suffered by being made the
of the Hegelian Idea, the empiricist spirit pays due regard to the importance
nality. Thirdly, room is made in philosophy for genuine religious experience,
t does not find expression in orthodox Christianity - as in the case of Eucken.
h religiously-minded empiricists rightly stress the importance of the
50).

II

he opinion of Robert Mackintosh, intuitionism "finds its chance in the mis-
es of empiricism" (251). Thus Reid and his followers appealed, against
scepticism, to the witness of conscience. Since "intuition" generally car-
h it the implication not only that things are so, but that they must be so,
osh feels justified in regarding intuitionalism as a half-way house between
sm and idealism. The intuitionalist considers that, unlike the empiricist,
nake room in his philosophy for moral ideals as well as for phenomenal
es. But for Mackintosh, intuitionalism provides no final resting-place. For
st resort it can only assert the primacy of the moral; it cannot justify it.
on an intuitionalist programme, we are left with a multiplicity of starting-
"Every percept is such a starting-point; it is an immediate certainty,
ng with us unmodified as the basis of reliable inference. Every First
e of the mind is a starting-point too" (252). Hence, for example, Reid's
d random" lists of first principles; hence too, the necessity of enquiring
idealism will furnish one all-embracing principle (253).

III

Mackintosh first administers an antidote to any in his day who were under
ession that British philosophy had ever been under the influence of idealism.
n that being the case, idealism, and especially that of the Platonic rather
Berkelian kind "is very generally strange to older British thinking." In

support of this he cites Austin's <u>Jurisprudence</u>, which explicitly assumes tha[t] dichotomy of utilitarian and intuitive theories in philosophy is exhaustive (254[).] Kant, however, we come to a philosopher whose subsequent influence upon B[ritish] thought has been considerable. Under his attack, the ultimacy of the percept[- the] conviction beloved of intuitionalists - is done away. Again, thought reacts up[on] sensation in order to produce the percept; otherwise we should never attain [to] experience - a goal which must for ever elude those who follow a strictly em[pirical] line. The "forms" of time and space are not derived from sensation; they ori[ginate] in the mind, and are presupposed in every experience. It is not open to man t[o] delineate the mechanics of the inter-actions of sensation, space-time, and th[ought.] But what of non-spatiotemporal objects such as God, world, and soul? Here, [says] Kant, speculative reason fails us, and that not merely because sense experie[nce] does not keep pace with thought's demands. Our dilemma is that we cannot pr[operly] regard the physical world as the real world, yet of that world alone we have k[now]ledge. Knowledge of reality being thus denied, man finds himself conscious n[one] less, of duty; and it is in moral, or practical experience that Kant locates th[e] remedy for scepticism. We shall trace further steps in Kant's thought when w[e turn] to natural theology. Enough has been said, however, to indicate the grounds o[n which] Mackintosh claims that

> "Kant ... has broken away from intuitionalism by substitutting <u>one system of necessity</u> for the many necessary truths or given experien[ces] from which intuitionalism takes its start ... (Yet) Kant's idealism is incomplete. On one side, the world we know by valid processes of thinking cannot, we are told, be the real world. Or, beginning from the other side; neither the reality which ideal thought reaches after, nor yet the reality which our conscience postulates, is the valid world of orderly thinking. The great critic of scepticism has diverge[d] from idealism towards scepticism again, or has given his idealism a sceptical colour, mitigated - but only mitigated - by faith in the mor[al] consciousness" (255).

Dr. Mackintosh detected no such wavering in Hegel, whose work "ranks, [in] our own day, as the last of the great philosophies, and the boldest of all" (256[). In it] we have the uncompromising declaration of the rationality of the universe, wh[ere] space, matter and nature are "proved" to be ascertainable and definable. The[n come] the outworkings of necessary truth in this system in which the element of give[nness,] dominant in empiricism, is sublimated. There is no dualism of fact and princ[iple:] things are as they <u>must</u> be. These convictions are expounded by means of Heg[el's] dialectic which "undertakes to show to candid minds that incompatible asserti[ons] not only may but must both be true" (257). Thus Hegel demonstrated to his ow[n sa]tisfaction that everything is necessarily as it is, and that everything is a cons[equence] of an ideal relationship.

Not all were as easily satisfied as Hegel himself. In <u>Hegel and Hegelianis[m]</u> Dr. Mackintosh reviewed Hegel's antecedents and successors, and dealt in so[me] detail with Hegel's logic; with the philosophies of nature and of spirit; with H[egel's] psychology, ethics and aesthetics; and with Hegelianism <u>vis à vis</u> history and [ ] Christianity. His concluding estimate of the system is, in the opinion of the p[resent] balanced and just, and we shall attempt a summary statement of it (258). ...osh welcomes Hegel's repulsion of Kantian scepticism, and his subtle use ...ncept of evolution in relation to knowledge. Hegel came to see evolution, ...formation, not so much as the working out of inevitability (as in intuitiona- ...ut rather as "the living process by which a mere germ of knowledge be- ...ransformed into a fully articulated organism" (259). However, Mackintosh ...t accept as adequate Hegel's dialectical method: he charged it with being ...where it was not paradoxical, and therefore the systematic coherence ...ought he had achieved was rendered perilously problematic. For his part ...osh desires to rescue the notion of the rationality of the real and of its ...to thought,

> "But we differ from Hegel in denying that this truth is the whole truth, adequate to the determination of the universe of being. The existence of a world of natural realities in time and space we do not think is genuinely deducible, though, when it is presented in experience, we can see that it is congruous to thought. And - what is still more important - the revelation of reality made in the philosophy of spirit is - to us men at least - something quite different from a set of new phases in the consciousness of an object. We must be in earnest in establishing a distinction between Divine and human consciousness. We must make the difficult assertion of the limitation of human knowledge and human experience" (260).

...ible is that Hegelianism knows too much. It "understands all mysteries" (261). ...however, its value is strictly limited. Christians, on the other hand, "know ...hich passes knowledge" (262). Hence idealists who deny this are as mis- ...s those sceptics who deny that we can know anything, and whose armour ...shattered by idealism's arrows.

> "The very significance of the weary moral discipline of life is that we are learning lessons from experience which mere "reason" on its "open field" - i.e. clever unspiritual intelligence - cannot conceivably master. Knowledge teaches us many short cuts; but a short cut which should supersede the significance of life has no charm to dazzle us" (263).

Mackintosh elsewhere affirmed, "The Christian religion is pre-eminently a ...rocess, and does not admit of being - at any rate by us men - reduced to ...f intellect" (264). It is even possible to adduce practical evidence of the ...ons of reason by reference to some who stand in the tradition of absolute ...:

> "in the name of ultimate reason - Professor Bradley gives us a Pantheistic Absolute, and no human immortality; and Dr. McTaggart gives us an eternal society of interrelated spirits, and no absolute being as such; and Professor Royce gives us God and immortality, but without mention of Christ; and Professor Taylor finds that Royce's arguments are vitiated by reliance upon the relational form of thought,

and himself gives us a fighting chance of immortality, and an Absolu
that cannot be called personal or a self. Such differences do not pro\
that idealism is barren; but surely they prove that idealism is no
case to claim a monopoly of certainty. Dim movements of faith may
be wiser than this shrill logical debate" (265).

IV

What then of the relations between philosophy and theology? Dr. Mackint(
aware that not all will find the study of theism to their taste. It is difficult; it
occupies that perilous borderland between philosophy and theology. In its eigh
century deistical form it seems temperamentally a long way from confident C
commitment to Christ. Nonetheless, "a thoroughgoing denial of natural theolc
usually proved a help to religious scepticism rather than to the assertion of r
tion" (266). We may approach Mackintosh's views on natural theology by mea
summary of his history of the subject, understanding by "natural theology" th
attempt to justify belief in God on rational grounds, and without recourse to r
tion (267). Though not denying the possibility of a natural theology, Mackintos
out that in practice few Christians have contented themselves with this, since
have testified to a greater revelation elsewhere. In practice, too, natural the
have been more concerned with the question of God's existence than of his nat
It was in order to redress this imbalance that A.B. Bruce in his <u>Apologetics</u>
equally one-sided in considering the latter question perhaps at the expense of
former (268). Bruce was exceptional in this, however, and our present purpo
will be met if we summarise Mackintosh's account of the history of the argum
for the existence of God.

The ontological argument is said to be "a system of idealistic philosophy
nutshell" (269). It is concerned to show that God, or the Absolute, necessaril
exists; that he necessarily is what he is; that he or it is necessarily manifest
that finite which we know from experience. Anselm propounded the first clear
of the argument, claiming that God necessarily exists because the perfection
includes existence is greater than a perfection confined to an object of thought
Despite its rejection by Aquinas the argument was later restated by Descartes
more attention now being paid to the notion of the necessary existence of the p
being. Spinoza's pantheistic determinism, with its emphasis upon the existenc
substance only, and his deductive reasoning to what <u>must be</u> displayed certain
methodological affinities with the ontological argument. Finally, Leibniz acce
the argument in qualified form.

Turning now from the <u>a priori</u> to the <u>a posteriori</u> type of argument we fin
the argument from design is the one which appeals most, though not exclusive
empiricist philosophers. It is found fairly frequently from Socrates onwards,
proceeds by analogy from the existence of designed organisms to the existenc
a designer. It will ever stop short of demonstrative proof, however, and at be
yields probability. Aquinas, following Albertus Magnus, refined it; Descartes
pudiated it; Butler appealed to it; and Paley provided the classic statement of

mological argument frequently, and notably in Aquinas, stands alongside the
nt from design - at least in the thought of those who are of an intuitionalist
han an empiricist cast of mind. Indeed Mackintosh goes so far as to say,
od or for evil, so far as there is an accepted line of theistic doctrine, that
is intuitionalist. Other schools of philosophy pay flying visits to theism;
ialism is at home there" (271). The arguments to a first cause, and to an
d mover come down to us from Aristotle; they are traceable in Philo of
ria, but come into their own with Aquinas. Wolff used the argument, and
no writer can be less intrinsically worthy of study than Wolff ... he is im-
as the man (together with Hume) against whom Kant directed his tremendous
' (272). Even Locke, who might have been expected to have shunned so in-
flavoured a doctrine, argued that God is the first great cause of the existence
minds.

h Kant we have in the first place the rejection of the above three arguments.
the prevailing tendency in theism he maintained that we have no right to
the three great arguments cumulatively:

"They offer alternatively and mutually exclusive conceptions of God.
If the God of the cosmological argument is "the Great First Cause,"
we have no right to identify him with the "Most real being" of the Ontological argument. If the God of the Design argument seems a limited
being, working as an artist upon given materials, he is hardly God at
all" (273).

h the ontological argument comes nearest to success it fails to prove God's
e, and merely shows that if we think of him as existing at all, we think of
necessarily existing. Secondly, and more positively, Kant propounded his
rgument for God's existence. We are driven to postulate a God who oversees
or moral ends. If, in Kant, this postulate was hedged about with sceptical
s - whilst we may know something of the mechanism of nature, can we be
it we are not cheated when we see moral purpose in it? - the idea was con-
adopted by later thinkers including Flint, who said, "we are conscious of
ependence" (274), thereby echoing one of the most attractive features in the
of Butler.

gel resuscitated the three traditional arguments in his own particular way,
ng them stages in the development of thought. As Mackintosh expresses it:

"This involves a re-interpretation of the Cosmological argument, or a
criticism of the view ordinarily taken of it. Trace out the clue of causation to the end, says Hegel in effect, and it introduces you, not to a
single first cause beyond nature, but to the totality of natural process -
a substance, as it were, in which all causes inhere. This is a sugges-
tion which deserves to be well weighed. The Design argument is held
to give a contrasted view. It suggests in very deed a personal but
limited God, or a number of Gods - "Religions of spiritual Individuality,"
including, along with "Judaism," the anthropomorphic religions of
Greece and Rome. Finally the Ontological argument sums up the truth
in the two previous arguments, and gives it worthier utterance in its

vision of the philosophical Absolute. This is the last word of religiou
truth, though pure philosophy stands still higher. And, in some sens(
not clearly explained, Hegel identifies this final religion with Christianity" (275).

The several arguments have subsequently appeared in various writers. Mill b
that the design argument led to a high degree of probability; Flint, without rel
Kant's case against taking the thought of God piecemeal, did exactly that in en
all four arguments to illustrate various attributes of God; Martineau's intuitic
gave great place to the a posteriori arguments; and Balfour relied upon a cru
form of the design argument, as follows:

"There must be a God, who could compel irrational matter to serve
rational ends - so ran the old argument. There must be a God who ca
miraculously endow the irrational mind of man with truth - so runs tl
new" (276).

To what conclusions did Dr. Mackintosh come as he reflected upon the hi:
natural theology? In the first place he accepts that Kant has dealt the death blc
the traditional grounds of belief in God. The three classical arguments will nc
up. Kant has shown decisively that the ontological argument is not really an a1
at all; that since it asserts uncaused causation even in the one instance of God
cosmological argument fails; and that the design argument could leave us with
a limited deity. Further, "the three cannot be strung on one thread, or provec
lead up to one and the same God, unless by the use of the inconclusive ontolog
argument ... Kant has broken (the old arguments) into little bits; and everyon
is competent to discuss the question ought to grant this" (277). Again, under F
hand the arguments became transformed into "reflections of the course of rati
thought in man" (278), and whatever else the Christian religion may be it is "ɪ
eminently a moral process, and does not admit of being ... reduced to terms
intellect" (279). Mackintosh claims that the old proofs have their value (thougl
does not precisely specify in what their value consists, and therefore he woulc
satisfy a latter-day humanist philosopher who might well inquire what value bɪ
signposts have!), but in the absence of revelation reason cannot make us sure
personal God, still less introduce us to his friendship (280). Nor will the trad
appeal to miracle help us. To any who might suggest the contrary Mackintosh
reply, "Would you believe any doctrine, whatever its moral complexion, if it :
miracles enough in its train? If you would, you are no Christian. If you would
then a certain amount of moral excellence is at any rate a sine qua non of reve
and in so far its evidence is partly internal" (281). In any case, the meaning o
gospel miracles is not exhausted when we have ascertained to the best of our a
that they actually occurred: "Miracles are useful if they bring a man face to fa
with Christ. If they do more they are misleading and hurtful" (282). In short,
not infer the divinity of Christ from the miracles he performed. Christian fait
not assent to the evidence of miracles. We believe "because of the moral glor;
God as seen by faith in the face of Jesus Christ" (283). We might express Mac
conviction in a nutshell by saying that miracles cannot be both signs to the bel:
and evidence offered to the sceptic. To suppose otherwise is to court circular:

ı anything of worth be salvaged from the wreck of natural theology? Mackin-
rtainly believes that we need a natural theology of some sort. It will necessar-
ıcomplete, but it may serve to lead men to the threshold of revelation. There
'elation, albeit dim and imperfect, of God's moral attributes in the material
ι. Hence, whilst natural theology does not yield proofs, it may offer sugges-
84). Further, from the Christian point of view, even if natural theology
spells out God's impersonal word "it is worth spelling over; all that comes
ɔd is sacred" (285). To this may be added man's knowledge of a moral law
e did not make, which he may violate, but which he cannot alter (286). Even
tiles, according to Paul in Romans, might have been expected to have been
ıf this (287). But when the worth of natural theology has been fully owned,
; has yet to be said. God has spoken in Christ. "We have a personal word
ɔd" (288). Thus the best evidence for the truth of Christianity is internal
e, not in the sense which presupposes an external, natural-theological type
ınce; but in the sense that "one cannot know what the Gospel of Jesus Christ
ıs one knows it from the inside" (289). Lying behind Mackintosh's thought
the Reformers' doctrine of the inner witness of the Holy Spirit; and it is
:ing to note that amidst much that might be branded "liberal" by latter-day
ns, we have here in Mackintosh an emphasis which many of them have been
make their own, and which some of them have somewhat incautiously ex-

may conclude then that Mackintosh firmly believes that God is revealed in
liwork; and that he is equally firmly persuaded that we cannot validly argue
s handiwork to God. It follows that metaphysics by no means conflicts with
to Christ. For example, even if natural theology were able to provide an
ionably valid demonstration of the existence of a God, this would not at all
ə or conflict with Christ's message, "The God for whom I speak desires and
ıs to be your friend ... does demonstration of a God-fact reveal God's
y heart towards us? Unless we make that foolish affirmation, Christianity
ınchallenged" (290). Whether or not there is a religious a priori, there
ı an ethical one as a postulate of faith. Conscience provides an independent
activity, and no matter what difficulties we may be involved in, we must
ırate intellectual from moral and religious considerations. They must ever
ʒht together. So, for example, despite the weaknesses of the cosmological
nt qua rational demonstration, "If there were nothing in this world which
look like God's world, faith would be too utterly a paradox" (291). Even
ırprising would be a state of affairs wherein it could be seriously maintained
l is to be found everywhere except in the religious experience (292). Hence,

"In nature we have a revelation of power, in conscience a revelation of
righteousness, and in Christ a revelation of love and redemption. In
nature we find suggestions of God; in conscience, the postulate of God;
in Christ, the affirmation of God. The lower elements of revelation are
all but lost apart from Christ; but Christ restores them to their true
meaning; and, in having Christ, we have God and His forgiveness. But
all moral revelation is twofold - a revelation of grace and of duty; a
revelation of moral forces above us, and of moral obligations resting
on us" (293).

But the words "grace" and "duty" herald our final chapter on theology and eth[ics]. Before turning to this, however, we may pause to sum up in his own words M[acin]tosh's understanding of the relations between Christianity and philosophy:

> "Christianity stands in a sense midway between the two types of philo[-] sophical religion - the morality whose God is incomplete, and the idealism whose infinite and absolute being is supermoral ... this is how one has learned Christ: We believe not only that "perfection is eternal" not only (in Bible language) that God's will is done already i[n] heaven by his holy angels; not merely, again, with the moralising people, that God's will may come to be done upon earth, as in heaven but that the battle has already been fought and won. Thus in Christ w[e] have not merely the possibility but the certainty of redemption, and not forgiveness alone but the new life. Life will not pass into us independently of our co-operation or against our will. But such powe[r] resides in Christ as ensures that the wedding shall be furnished with guests; and the power avails for every willing heart. So we say not simply, "All may yet be well," but "All must be well." ... And so w[e] still preach Jesus as Lord and as Saviour; to the Pragmatist a stumb[l-] ing block and to the Idealist foolishness; but to them who are called, whether from the one camp or the other, Christ the power and the wi[s-] dom of God. This is more than our theology; it is our gospel. Woe b[e] to us if we desert it, because this or that school of philosophy, or, i[f] it be so, all philosophy finds it anomalous! The foolishness of God is wiser than men.
>
> ... we must insist upon this - that Christian theology is not yet mediatized, or retired upon a pension, or a suppliant for the crumbs from the philosophical banquet. Christ is still king in the kingdom of God: the Son who alone knows the Father, or who alone can communi· cate the revelation to others. Philosophy, however well disposed, an[d] however competent in its own sphere, must not lay down the law to Christian doctrine; which strives to answer the other, the immense question, <u>What thinkest thou of Christ</u>? (294)

CHAPTER V

THEOLOGY AND ETHICS
———————————

[O]f the necessity of theology Robert Mackintosh had no doubt. Personal faith may [suffice t]he individual Christian, but the Church needs dogmatic theology: "a scienti[fic acco]unt, so far as attainable, of its spiritual wealth; and this in the interests both [of un]ity and of <u>completeness</u> of spiritual experience" (295). Mackintosh is aware [that] the term "scientific" in a special sense here. He has in mind theology's [effort] to make for order, coherence, and system, and to provide grounds of some [of its] religious claims. At the back of his mind, too, is the notion of scientific [method] which he feels the theologian should emulate as he reconstructs theology, [drops] outworn dogmas, and sifts and tests the statements of theology and apolo[getics (2]96). Though important, however, theology is secondary and reflective: [faith] is primary. "A religious man need no more be a theologian than a poet need [know the] theory of aesthetics" (297). As contrasted with the certitude of religious faith, [the bes]t theology can aim at is probability, approximation. Its results possess vali[dity and] importance in proportion as they have a practical bearing.

Mackintosh avers that historically (and, presumably, natural theology [apart) C]hristian theology has developed as a doctrine concerning Christ. For Christ [is conce]ived as the redeemer, and therefore it is his relation to God and to man [which is] pivotal. In the activity of the God-man we have the high peak of divine re[velation.]

> "Christian theology is not a speculative Theism; is is a doctrine of
> redemption. In other words, it does not furnish a theory of the Divine
> causation as such, but of Divine grace, or of those processes by which
> God works out the redemption of guilty man" (298).

[There i]s an essential exclusiveness about Christianity from which Mackintosh does [not shri]nk. "Apart from Christ, the intuition of God is not to be had ... Communion [with Go]d is possible only on God's initiative; and Christ it is who leads us into fel[lowship] with God" (299). No emasculating Victorian theological liberalism here! [Here is] a Barthian before Barth. Since the sentences just quoted appear to consort [with] Mackintosh's views on natural theology, we must understand by "God" in the [above] context the Christian Father-God. Whatever other knowledge of God there [may be,] there is no "saving and blessed knowledge of God elsewhere, but only in [Jesus C]hrist" (300). The sharp edge of this truth has been blunted, he feels, by [the Ch]ristian mystics in the interests of all-embracing love. Whilst this is par[donable] as a reaction against the more grotesque excesses of Augustinian and Cal[vinist] theology, we must ever remember that

> "No Bible writer tells us that humanity, as a natural whole, is in
> saving touch with God. We are told that salvation is God's gift, and
> that the gift is made through Jesus Christ - not through some vague
> general revelation of love. We owe the mystics much in the way of

parable, symbol, poetry; but they must not be taken as the final
authority in religion. For Christians, that place belongs only to
Christ" (301).

One imagines that Mackintosh redivivus would make the same point against ce
contemporary theologians: "Men who dislike (the claim that the God who works
where imparts himself only through Christ) may abandon Christianity ... But
have a right to remodel Christianity, or to alter the terms of the Divine mess
(302). Christ himself is part of the message, and we cannot separate the reve
from the revealer (303). On the other hand, Mackintosh's intensely moral app
to theology caused him agonies not only, as we have seen, with the harsher fo
of predestinarian doctrine, but also with the grim possibility that the good Go(
should commit the vast majority of mankind, pre-Christian and non-Christian
eternal ruin solely on account of their not possessing the Christian revelation,

> "When we compare the revealed character of God with the ocean tor-
> rent of human souls which has been passing for ages into the unseen
> world, it becomes morally certain that God has other agencies in the
> employment of His Gospel besides those which are visibly at work on
> earth. Yet we have nothing directly to do with these – of whatever
> kind they may be. We have to be faithful to our own calling in the Kin
> dom of God" (304).

As to our account of what we do know, Mackintosh was quite sure that theologi
statement was in dire need of revision. Theological method which relies upon
ference will not suffice; natural theology is incomplete; a priori theological c
structions do not touch us deeply; and confessional theology imposes burdens
ous to be borne. What is the alternative? "We are persuaded that faith knows
not by inference, but by beholding His glory, full of grace and truth. Not at se
hand, but at first hand, we know our Lord and Master. He calls us; we follow
(305). He is aware that he will at this point incur the charge of subjectivity, b
remains convinced that "incommunicable personal experience is the only 'firn
foundation of Christian faith' "(306). It follows that the Christian cannot prove
can but testify.

Mackintosh acknowledges theology's debt to the eighteenth century evange
who "in judging of doctrines by their practical and experimental significance .
while receding from the traditional orthodoxy, have spiritually made a great a
and have laid hold of the very key to theology" (307). Unfortunately, they did r
work out the idea very systematically. Nevertheless their principle of the reli
consciousness is "the formative principle which will reconstruct theology in tl
few years or decades" (308). The matter is summed up in the following lyrica
sage:

> "The final authority cannot be anything without; it must be a voice
> within. It cannot be the most august or even the dearest human autho
> rity; it must be God Himself bearing witness by His Spirit to His Son
> This is the legitimate prolongation of the evidence of history and of
> the Church's witness; this interprets to us all that has gone before.
> Conscience is our final court of appeal; conscience is the absolute

master of our days, whose service sets us free. Christian evidence reaches us in fulness then, and only then, when God reveals His Son in us, and conscience lays down its authority at Christ's feet - when God shines into our hearts, to show us His glory in the face of Jesus Christ. Thus we see the Father and are satisfied" (309).

) important corollaries of this position require to be stated. Firstly, whilst e that "the Christian life must be known from the inside, or it is not known 310), and whilst the Christian can prove nothing to others by appealing to his ıce, we may not assent to Lotze's view that "religious truth is credible be-
: its intrinsic value - because it ought to be true. This would imply that al revelation is needless and illusory" (311). Nothing could be further from ı. The Christian faith is historically anchored, and the "disposition to weed ontingent historical facts from the content of Christian faith, and to confine eternal ideal principles" (312) is unacceptable. Doubtless this leaves us with ons which, technically, are probable only and not proven, but, for example, :ansfer Christian evidence from the "historical" to the "philosophical" with dall - we surely cut down Christianity to the limits of theism" (313). This he question of the reliability of the gospel narratives, and in his last book, ∍ntral Things, Mackintosh argued for their general trustworthiness. The n has the subjective certainty of something objectively done.

ɔndly, the appeal to Christ as known to Christian consciousness rules out of y lesser allegiances - whether to creeds, councils, or even to the Bible. No is to be found in any of these; and if to commit oneself to Christ in the ab-
' external confirmatory evidences is to run a risk, it is also to "run so as to (314).

"There are not two kinds of Christian faith, one of which believes in Christ to the soul's salvation, while the other believes the accuracy of Scripture wholesale and undigested. It is with God that we have to do, and with Jesus Christ, the image of the invisible God, and the only way of access to the Father. Our certainty stands in our recognising Christ's voice and following Him. People ask for an objective standard of spiritual truth, apart from the moral state of their hearts. They ask for it, but God will never give it. They pretend to possess it in the Church; and God allows the Church to grow foul with corruption that their idol may be broken. They pretend to possess it in the Bible; and God sets all the microscopes of critical research to scrutinise the Bible, that every flaw may be made the most of. What is the orthodox claim but idolatry? 'We cannot do with the invisible God. Give us something nearer at hand to revere.' And, like every superstition, it claims to be far more devout than spiritual faith. Did they not call the early Christians atheists?" (315)

I

Robert Mackintosh touched upon many theological topics in his numerous writings. Characteristically, his own convictions tend to emerge in the cours[e of] his criticisms of others, and few themes are fully developed. Even the atonem[ent] upon which he wrote much, is dealt with in this way, and <u>Historic Theories of Atonement</u> leaves us with a brief "tentative construction" only. It is not that Mackintosh lacked ability, but rather that confronted by such mighty themes reverence and humility caused him to shrink from speaking any word which m[ight] be taken to be final. If we take the trouble, however, to classify his scattered utterance under various headings, we find perfectly clear and consistent tende[ncies] in his thought. We shall attempt this task, beginning with Mackintosh's unders[tand]ing of God.

Robert Mackintosh was a trinitarian. In his view the Holy Spirit is the Sp[irit of] Christ, and is best regarded as the one who takes the things of Christ and she[ws] them to us (316). Christ himself was never mere man, as Ritschlianism wron[gly] supposed (317). He was sinless, and his life may be regarded as a great act o[f] self-sacrifice for sinners. But this implies that in a pre-existent state of bles[sed]ness he willed to make such an offering. Hence there follows the conception o[f] kenosis - Christ emptied himself both of blessedness and of divine predicates:

> "This doctrine of Kenosis remains the necessary <u>Vorstellung</u> by whi[ch] our ignorance expresses two moral facts - that Christ in self-sacrificing love, came to us out of the divine glory, and that Christ's hum[an] love would not endure to be baulked of true and complete humanity ev[en] by shreds adhering to Him from the Divine glory itself" (318).

On the other hand, when introducing a discussion of Dr. R.S. Franks's paper [" Person of Christ in the Light of Modern Scholarship" (319), he felt bound to a[gree] with Franks "that we run great risks if we identify the Christian cause with th[at] of Kenosis. ... Although the <u>word</u> Kenosis comes from St. Paul, it is in the l[ast] degree improbable that the apostle - though he doubtless taught a Pre-existen[t] Christology - had come face to face with the perplexities of modern orthodoxy regarding the transition of a Divine being from the fulness of heavenly knowle[dge] to earthly limitations. In St. Paul, Kenosis probably just means "self-sacrific[e]" (320).

These pneumatological and Christological considerations, together with t[he] understandings of God which stress his roles of creator and father, are summ[ed] for Mackintosh in the doctrine of the Trinity. Having regard to his attitude tov[ards] credal definition, we are not surprised to discover that Mackintosh does not c[oncern] himself with mere assent to formulae in this connection. On the contrary, he questions "whether men are entitled to the exact definitions of Greek theology, whether these have any meaning" (321). One root of the Athanasian doctrine o[f the] Trinity is metaphysical: it constitutes an attempt to speculate upon God's self-consciousness and upon his essential nature as love. This attempt fails for th[ree] reasons. There is firstly the question of the <u>inscrutability</u> of God's nature, an[d] secondly, the difficulty of passing from the Trinitarian process to the Second Hypostasis. Finally, there is the fact that "the (ecclesiastical) doctrine of the

)t taught in the N.T. and cannot be got from the N.T. by any fair expository
;, and therefore cannot be reckoned among truths necessary for salvation
abandoning the great Protestant thesis of the sufficiency of Scripture, and
incurring the condemnation pronounced on those who "teach for doctrines
mandments of men" "(322).

) other root of Athanasian trinitarian doctrine is religious and practical,
is the one Mackintosh would stress. The doctrine of the Trinity presents
d truths:

"God is our Father; Christ is the only way to God; though absent from
us now in His earthly humanity, Christ is still with us in Spirit, and,
through Christ, God is with us - such is the New Testament doctrine
of the Trinity; a doctrine altogether practical, everywhere in contact
with the religious life of men" (323).

e proceed to enquire to what end the nature and purpose of God are made
o man the answer given is "for the redemption of sinful humanity;" and here,
ng with Mackintosh's view that historically theology has been largely con-
with the person and work of Christ, we approach those themes which he
ntral in his thinking.

II

en the evolutionary model came to be applied to morality, many found fertile
the propagation of the idea that moral progress was somehow as inevitable
evolution in other spheres. Some secularists and some (especially popular)
s writers canvassed the idea that with an improved environment man would
e easily tread the upward path upon which he was, in any case, set. A re-
tion, current in certain quarters, was that of the perfectibility of man - a
ity ardently entertained by Condorcet. It is true, as Elliott-Binns has pointed
), that Huxley dealt the death blow to the idea of mechanical progress, and
; weakened the moral analogy somewhat; and also that the difference between
's optimistic <u>First Principles</u> and his subsequent <u>Principles of Sociology</u>
onds to a real change in the mental atmosphere. But at the popular level of
pew and platform liberal moral optimism remained a considerable force (325).
)elief in the inevitability of man's moral progress there frequently went a
;ing of the importance of the fact of sin. Thus, for example, Hegelianism led
iedermann (1819-1885) to the conclusion that God could not be both Absolute
sonal; and that in fact he was Absolute. But this entailed that there could be
thing as sin, understood as the violation of a <u>personal</u> relationship with God.
e other side, Ritschl had regarded sin as a matter of individual failure: man
realise ethical values, and this is sin. Not for him the notion of an estranged
an affronted, holy and righteous God. Between these extremes stands
osh, embracing neither a glibly easy liberal optimism, nor an hyper-Cal-
despair of non-elect mankind.

For Dr. Mackintosh, "sin is no mere defect. It is a virulent cancer. It b₁
with it guilt, which destroys the soul's inner peace, and frightens it away fror
It mars and distorts that growth of character which is the chief end of human l
and of the history of the race" (326). It is part of the ministry of Christ to ma
this plain to us. "He reveals our malady as not weakness or accident but guilt
Moreover, the sin in which the individual is involved is social and not simply
sonal. The "frequent choice of evil on the part of the race has dislocated its r
to God. Though communion with God is not abolished, it is indefinitely weaken
(328). Although the individual is not guilty except by his own personal bad choi
and whilst "a guilty infant is a contradiction in terms" (329), there exist none
less on the one hand the moral claim of freedom, and on the other hand, the n
fact of the world's sin (330). These principles have to be held together, but th
must not be so held as to imply the intolerable doctrine of total inability. "In ₁
of fact, men, depraved as they are, have not become as wicked as possible" (
and even Calvinism had to take account of the freedom of the will as indicative
"capacity to be saved." Paradoxically, nothing did more to preserve this teac
in face of the ultra-logical Calvinistic confessionalism of the eighteenth centu₁
that "Half-Christianity" Deism, which proclaimed God's universal immanence
The moral is that "we must beware of describing the natural history of sin in
which will not commend itself to men's consciences as being true to fact" (33₈
again, "the world's sporadic goodness must be precious in the sight of the wo₁
Saviour" (334).

III

Given the fact of the sin of the individual and of the race, how is reconcili
with God to be achieved? As we might expect Mackintosh rules out of court an
of Pharisaism. Works will not save us; legalism has nothing to offer in this n
Whereas Jesus was faithful to the spirit of the Old Testament Law whilst trans
ing its letter, the Pharisees kept the letter and destroyed the Law's spirit. "C
the gracious faith of patriarchs and psalmists, they developed an immense ca₅
cal machinery of self-salvation. And with this they galvanised their dead relig
into an appearance of life for centuries" (335). The studies of the late T.W. ℕ
and others, suggest that this assertion is somewhat bald. There was a warme
more ethical side to Pharisaic and rabbinic Judaism. But in so far as it is tru
"for Jesus good living is the spontaneous activity of a transformed character;
the Scribes and Pharisees it is obedience to a discipline imposed from without
Mackintosh is right to sound a warning note. And his main point to the effect t
vation is by grace rather than by works cannot be gainsaid by any serious stu₍
the New Testament, wherein the sole condition of forgiveness is that we confe
sin (337). Despite this, legalism has reared its head on numerous occasions i₁
Christian history. In the Westminster Shorter Catechism, for example, the a₁
to Question 85 suggests that God demands three things of sinners: faith, plus ₁
ance; plus churchgoing. "We are faced by an angry God; and His anger is "du
us for sin. Yet this angry God will lift his curse from off us - on terms. He w
accept a composition. He is prepared to bargain" (338). The tragedy is that th

Puritan could not conceive of a "moral order which is not a legal order; (of
a reward which is not a legal reward, excluding the operation of grace" (339).
ult for the believer was that

> "doctrinally and emotionally he was to live by grace; but his conduct was
> to be exactly the same <u>as if he expected to be justified by works</u>. ...
> The sacrament of the Lord's Supper, instead of being the centre of
> Christian fellowship, as in the early Church, was to be a rare and
> exceptional privilege. ... Before receiving the sacrament, one must
> 'examine' himself; not, as the Apostle meant, to remind oneself of
> what he was doing and what he might hope to gain - but in order to
> ascertain whether he was legally perfect. This self-examination was
> to be regularly accompanied by humiliation and fasting. At service
> after service the Christian should hear the law of God ringing his
> death-knell - "The soul that sinneth, it shall die - it shall die!" Until
> finally, when he had been brought very low - almost as low as before
> he became a 'believer' and a 'professor' - then, at the eleventh hour,
> it was allowed to come to him, as a happy thought, that there <u>was</u>
> such a thing as grace with God" (340).

osh grants that this system did breed some strong and tender men. He further
hat

> "had God been pleased to ordain that sinners should work their way
> to heaven through a purgatory of legal bondage, even under the reign
> of Christ, who of us could have dared to impeach either the justice,
> or the mercy, or the wisdom of God's doing so? But, if God has
> chosen to do the opposite, and if He has appointed that holiness shall
> triumph over sin just in proportion as men receive free forgiveness,
> and carry about God's peace with them, who are men, even the holiest,
> that they should re-edit the gospel of the grace of God" (341)?

i's free grace in Christ alone which saves. Hence a doctrine of atonement
sought which does no violence to this cardinal fact of Christian experience.

re are other, equally important facts with which a satsifactory atonement
must square. It must not, on the one hand, play down the historicity of the
Christ as do some "fanatics of the Rationalist Press - those light-armed
hers of unbelief" (342); and as even some Christians do, who are "engrossed
hrist idea and indifferent to the Christ fact" (343). On the other hand, a
of atonement is misnamed if it teaches that the fact of Christ's death is the
of the doctrine. To say that Jesus died is not the same as saying that "Christ
sin by the sacrifice of himself" (344); yet this latter is what an atonement
must say, and it will find a response only in the experience of those who
the tragedy of Calvary was morally necessary. If it were otherwise, and if
no need to express itself in suffering, "is that which suffers love, or is it
(345) Further, in some way or another, a worthy doctrine of atonement
count for the fact that "Atonement was necessary not merely in order that
ght be truly man but that God might be God" (346). Older orthodox theology
claim that God "might justly" have left man to his ruin. But Mackintosh

avers that God would not have been true to his name as love "had He contented
self with constitutional excuses for inaction" (347). Along what lines, then, di
Mackintosh think - albeit tentatively - a satisfactory atonement doctrine could
constructed?

IV

We may say in the first place that Mackintosh understood the atonement t
in some sense, an objective necessity, and that it was made a practical possi
by the once-for-all death of Christ. Thus, for example, he expressed the sus
that the COPEC Report was on dangerous ground in appearing to suggest that
Christians are in some way to prolong and complete the process of atonement
the contrary, the atonement is Christ's finished work (348). And it really hap
Hence his despair over R.C. Moberly whom he quotes as follows:

> "It is to Calvary, not as ourselves but as Calvary, that in the
> breaking up of ourselves we most earnestly desire to hold fast. We
> are left, here at least and now, still gazing as from afar, not in
> fruition but in faith, on that which we have not realized in ourselves.
> We are still kneeling to worship, with arms outstretched from our-
> selves in a wonder of belief and loving adoration, that reality wholly
> unique and wholly comprehensive, the Figure of Jesus crucified" (34

On all of which Mackintosh comments:

> "One feels as if one were worshipping in some thronged crypt, dark
> with stained glass, the air heavy with incense, where sacred rites ar
> performed by an emaciated priest, who is bowed with sorrow almost
> to the ground. The whole scene is exquisitely beautiful, but crushing
> in its sadness. Then, as we close the High Church volume, and open
> the New Testament, our eyes light upon such words as these: "I writ
> unto you, My little children, because your sins are forgiven you for
> His name's sake." We are in the fresh air! We are in the sunshine!
> We are in the presence of a loving God, of a victorious Saviour! How
> much better God's sunshine is than the Church's crypt" (350)!

All that was necessary has been done. It is not the case, of course, that the a
was absolutely necessary behaviour on God's part - "that would be a gnosis in
The Atonement is absolutely necessary for us, not for God. Or the Atonement
hypothetically necessary in the divine administration; it is necessary on the h
thesis that man is to be saved" (351). On this ground Mackintosh affirms that
ever upholds the necessity and the sufficiency of Christ's death is intellectual
Christian (352). But the crucial question is, "What is the nature of this necess
and how is Christ sufficient?"

Mackintosh is the first to grant that objective theories of atonement may l
stated in offensive, immoral terms. After reviewing historic theories of this
he concluded that almost all of them give the impression that the necessity of

nt consists in the need for a device for unlocking the gate to God's forgiveness cy (353). This is particularly true of those theories which deny both the nd the Son by asserting that "there is no grace in God till Christ's death sfied justice'," (354) and which rely upon the abhorrent (to Mackintosh) of penal substitution.

penal substitutionary theory receives searching criticism at Mackintosh's 55). Firstly, he questions whether we may properly speak of punishment as g justice. Punishment may vindicate justice, or reassert it against the er, "but it cannot put him right with justice" (356). Secondly, most Old nt scholars grant that sacrifice did not denote penal substitution, and the al metaphors of the New Testament testify to the fact of Christ's atoning t do not define a theory concerning it. It is therefore irresponsible on the nyone to claim that the penal substitutionary theory is clearly derivable scriptures. Thirdly, the theory offends our religious consciousness: we el, when in a relationship with God, that but for a miraculous, tempera- uirk, he might justly have condemned us. That is, God is not "essentially and accidentally or contingently loving, gracious, redemptive" (357). Fourth- heory cannot explain how forgiveness leads to a life of obedience. We might, be grateful that a substitutionary arrangement has been made on our behalf, gratitude cannot be regarded as the fount of new life: that remains an arbi- tion of the Holy Spirit. Further, since the notion of transferred punishment (358), we are supposed to be thankful that in our case morality has been ed! Fifthly, the penal substitutionary theory raises many logical difficulties, concerning the "battle of Divine attributes" (359). The Father and the Son over against each other, the one condemning the innocent, the other yielding ding.

evangelical Arminianism help us out of the impasse? Is it the case that red to save men but could not legally do so unless or until Christ bore the of our sin? Mackintosh thinks not, and his chief objection to this notion is ivorces Christ from the gift of the Holy Spirit. On the theory in question sal- ay be attributed to the Father or to the Spirit, "but Christ appears only as oncluded certain necessary preliminary arrangements involved in the plan of " (360). Again, if

"the God of the Calvinist, who deliberately foreordains His creatures to eternal sin and eternal misery, is ... morally incredible ... the God of the evangelical Arminian, whose will is divided against His own nature, - who does His utmost to redeem the human race, and reluctant- ly sees men ... going on to a certain eternity of sin and misery - such a God is intellectually hard to conceive" (361).

he last resort, and for all their merits, purely objective theories of the nt claim too much. They do not pause before mystery. After all,

"it is hardly conceivable that this holy mystery should be made intel- ligible by the use of the methods of the market or the law court. One has a painful feeling that Christianity presents no darkness to the intellect of Quendstedt, or Calixtus, or Owen, or Jonathan Edwards. Whisper the word imputation in the scholastic sense, the darkness of the intellect is dispersed as by magic. That the sunshine of the heart (362) is dispersed at the same time I dare not affirm; yet I think the sky must be a good deal overcast when the divine procedure has been exposed to so vulgarizing an interpretation" (363).

Fortunately the fact is greater than the theories about it, and "even after the matists have spoken their last and worst word, God remains wonderful" (364) all, "Something came to pass in Christ's death, apart from which God had not duly glorified nor man redeemed" (365).

Will purely subjective theories serve us any better? Hardly; and certainl far as Moral Influence theories are concerned, their abiding difficulty has bee they cannot genuinely make room for moral necessity. The atonement may we from one point of view, the presupposition of the redemption of human charac but much more needs to be said. Dr. Mackintosh states his case so well that not forbear to quote at length:

"Enlightenment, emotion, impulse are natural psychological events which any one man may happen to produce in another man's mind. Such events do not need for their origination a Son of God humbling Himself and becoming obedient to death on the cross. If such events are the whole of what Christianity means, the Apostle Paul's reducti ad absurdum is the last word in the matter; then Christ died gratuit- ously. It is with these theories as with much apologetic preaching. Ir vain shall we talk to men from the pulpit about the refinement of man ners, about the growth of philanthropic organisations. These are not the characteristic work of Christ. Others have been reformers and social pioneers; they have their reward and their due honour. There is nothing of Gethsemene and Calvary in their work. To praise Christianity for the wrong things is not to support it, but to under- mine it. .... He who has only subjective views of the Atonement (in the above sense at least) is intellectually not a Christian; and though his heart may be better than his head, or his meaning than his inter- pretation of it, he will act as a pulverising or solvent force on Christian belief; and those he forms, if they have nothing else to go upon, will be likely to drop that objective Christianity to which he ma have been personally faithful. If you are to preach Christ with effect, you must preach salvation. A Christ who has no functions except Addisonian essays and gentle moral suasion, is not a Christ. The de of such a Christ has no appreciable meaning, and He will have no ap- preciable meaning to us when we are on our deathbeds" (366).

In the light of this quotation we may readily understand the zeal with whic Mackintosh sought to run subjective theories to ground when they were submit him for review. A single example will suffice: C.J. Cadoux's The Message A the Cross. According to Mackintosh, "One might have thought it impossible to a thinner version of the Moral Influence theory than the Dean of Carlisle's (36

t conceive that our own theologian (368) has done this" (369). The nub of the
m is that when Cadoux speaks of "the Saviourhood of every disciple," and so
minimises the uniqueness of what Christ has done. Further, whereas Cadoux
that it is by the blood of the saints that the world is redeemed, Mackintosh
s No! it is by the blood of the Lamb; and concludes that "the modern teaching
near indeed to a denial of the Lord that bought us" (370).

is Mackintosh is led to seek a way between objectivism of the Calvinistic kind
ne hand, and the subjectivism of the Moral Influence school on the other. He
ns the objective moral necessity of the atonement as the precondition of sinful
alvation, and affirms that no atonement theory can be considered satisfactory
oes not meet the requirements that glory be done to God's character as love,
: due emphasis be accorded to Christ's once-for-all act of redemption. At the
me, a satisfactory theory will make room for the appropriation by faith on
istian's part of the forgiveness and new life which the Cross makes available.

> "Thy love unknown
> Has broken every barrier down."
> The barriers were no dream, no hallucination. Their removal also,
> thank God, is no hallucination, but the very life by which we live.
> Whether we can fully explain either the barriers or their removal
> is another question.... I wish to be perfectly clear about the distinc-
> tion between a theory of the facts, even if it should be a true theory,
> and the great central certainty itself ... we see here and now in a
> glass, darkly; yet He whom we see is God our Saviour" (371).

V

t how many thus see? Are there few or many that be saved? Implicit in
tosh's understanding of penal substitution and in his dissatisfaction with the
y of the Westminster Confession generally, is his hostility towards any
iderstanding of electing grace, and, especially, towards the doctrine of
predestination. He can understand how this latter doctrine arises. Paul,
to account for the elective nature of God's dealings with Israel, finds in
ination the key to the solution of the problem. "But the truth is, that this
bye-path, had he continued in it, would have proved as fatal to the apostle's
nt, and therefore to his peace of mind, as it has proved to the peace of mind
r of his readers" (372).

> "If we frame the evil dogmas, that some are saved and some lost,
> and that the difference is due to God's own choice; that the saved are
> saved because God willed their salvation, while the lost perish be-
> cause He preferred their perdition; that the difference between one
> and another is due to God's arbitrary preference, or else to some
> hidden motive; so that even the Christian, if Predestinationism is
> true, worships an unknown and probably unknowable God, not a God
> of love: then, alas,

> The pillared firmament is rottenness
> And earth's base built on stubble.

There is perhaps no result more unexpected from the study of the Christian doctrine of Atonement, but certainly none is better assured than that Predestinationism - God's unmotived or secret will, used a the master-key - always works for the disintegration both of theology and of faith. ... It is time that Christian theology should cease to dabble in blasphemy" (373).

As he elsewhere expresses it, this time in connection with the Shorter Catech

> "Though Calvinists do recognise what they term "sovereign" love, yet, in the Catechism we never read that God so loved the world - only that He chose to save the elect. At this point then Calvinism almost inevitably enthrones Caprice as supreme in the universe - supreme even in redemption.... The doctrine known as "particular redemption" admits of nothing better" (374).

We must not suppose, however, that in forsaking predestinarianism Dr.] tosh rushes headlong into universalism. He is much too cautious for that, and too profound a grasp of the meaning of those scriptural passages which undoub indicate the urgency of decision, and the folly of prevarication. Again, he stee middle course: "That our Theodicy includes the affirmation of universal salva do not believe. But it includes the affirmation of God's universal will to save" His theodicy also has an unmistakable Irenaean flavour in so far as he speaks terms of man's probation, and sees it as compatible with this that there shoul extraterrestrial possibilities of hearing the Gospel - otherwise what of all tho could not, because of lack of opportunity, respond to God's grace in Christ? I no abandonment of God's moral purpose if he should make some provision for but there would be something morally distasteful, to say the least, in a God w have made such a provision and did not (376). But still, we dare not legislate will in fact be saved, and we can by no means predict the number of those who or will not:

> "We believe that the choice is real - life or death. And whatever be t form of the fate that awaits the obdurately impenitent - dimly but dre fully shadowed in Scriptural metaphors - we have no reason but to believe that it is possible for character to be irretrievably ruined, and the soul for ever lost" (377).

This is what we should expect, given that God is righteous love. "God's love i mere benevolence. He will judge sin because He loves righteousness.... Grac cludes morality within itself; love is justice at white heat" (378).

If a worthy doctrine of atonement will not open to view the "mechanics" o1 "arithmetic" of salvation, the appropriation by faith of the benefits of salvatio should certainly make for newness of life. On this point Mackintosh is insister The difference between a Christian and his non-Christian neighbour is that wh the latter lives by choice, the former lives by grateful obedience; but obedien a child-like, rather than a legalistic, kind. He lives in response to a God who

grace; he lives to appropriate what God gives. But what is given is by no
salvation of an individualistic kind. The new relationship with God in which
istian lives is necessarily social. "Personal salvation is not a selfish mat-
rist is revealed in all the New Testament - whatever the logic of Calvinism
le of Him - as the Saviour of the world; and no one who enters on the blessed
ice of God's mercy chokes the way of access for others; he rather clears it"
The burden of Dr. Mackintosh's complaint against much evangelical revivalism
t it was so weak at this point. "Evangelicalism, for the most part, has been
parasite. It has presupposed that "the world" will keep the wheels of the
nachine running, and has confined itself to the interests of its own or its
ur's soul" (380). It has done nothing for business life, for politics, for
, or for art. It has been found "blaspheming every discovery in turn, "talk-
eitfully for God" with more than Jesuitical tortuousness, and with vastly less
suitical skill" (381). A true Christianity, by contrast, will have a word to
nd an example to show in the world of men as it is. Hence, finally, to ethics.

VI

:ording to Dr. Mackintosh, "the Christian (ethical) motive is thankfulness for
ing love. And personal love to our Lord incorporates love towards all the
rinciples for which he stands" (382). The Christian's motive in ethical activi-
is different from that of the non-Christian. This is why, for the forseeable
Christian and philosophical ethics must stand apart (383). On the other hand,
ciple of natural law makes for a real measure of common ground between
ins and others, and witnesses to an objectivity which Mackintosh deems to
rucial to ethics as to atonement theology. We must not suppose that Mackin-
uld espouse a natural law theory according to which, from basic principles,
ogical deductions as to appropriate courses of action in particular cases could
e. His use of the notion is rather as a counter to subjective relativism in ethics,
in explanation of the fact that there is manifestly moral activity on the part
qua man, and irrespective of his religion or lack of it. He further feels that
the universal phenomenon of conscience, which bears witness to <u>duty</u> as
)mething over against the individual. "Whether he hears the voice of con-
distinctly or indistinctly ... man knows that he is subject to a law which he
make, which he can indeed violate, but which he cannot alter. Duty is the
gnificant factor in human experience" (384).

e of the practical implications of this view is that individuals have real moral
ibility; they are morally accountable. Thus Mackintosh has no patience with
agnoses of offenders which suggest that "somebody else" is always respon-
r what the offender did. He contends that by such sentimental means we
te the offender's personality and "lull tempted souls into a deadly security"
The responsibility for which he fights, however, is not merely a postulate
s, but of theology too. Christian ethics postulates both a God who has made
known in Christ, and a mankind which, possessing freedom and responsi-
louts God and sins. "No individual act of sin is necessitated" (386). On the

79

other hand, no virtue is at its completest until achieved in Christ, in whom al the highest source of value is to be found. Dr. Mackintosh's penultimate book Values, both lays bare his axiological assumptions and also provides him with platform for some of his judgements upon society and morals. The following i gist of his position.

Mackintosh seeks to isolate a number of value spheres, and treats first o economic values. Under this heading he is particularly suspicious of those wh would overthrow old-established values in the interest of socialism. He charg Christian Socialists with branding industrial freedom "selfishness and greed" In fact, he claims, self-interest is not always selfish and greedy, and can pro service to the community.

> "There are other devils besides those which preoccupy our Socialist Christians. Mankind as a race is lazy and mankind as a race is stupi If you refuse to allow self-interest the opportunities to which it is reasonably entitled, you will bring in no reign of 'altruism' but rathe an orgy of stupidity and an orgy of laziness. Not laziness but industr not stupidity but efficiency; is required both for economic and for moral welfare in any society. And if moral values are to carry the day - is freedom of no significance, morally?" (388)

In a somewhat aristocratic-prophetic tone Mackintosh goes on to accuse the n Christian Socialists of perpetrating highly undesirable semantic changes in the interest of their cause: "spite does not cease to be spite, or sin to be sin, by ducing itself as "the psychology of the working classes" "(389).

Turning to hedonism, Mackintosh finds that this cannot account for the m fact of life that sometimes experiences which we would claim have the greates for us, cannot at all be assessed in terms of the degree of pleasure which the promote. On the contrary, they may be sombre, yet sacred (390). Ritschl's p is hardly more satisfactory than that of an outright hedonist, for he tries to cl all spiritual experiences of the human mind on a psychological model:

> "The thesis implied, though not fully worked out, is that all values, the highest as well as the lowest, are sensed subjectively as pleasure We are very nearly back to hedonism; though we are spared the auda cious dogma that valuableness means pleasureableness and nothing besides ... (Ritschl's) assertions are correct but trivial ... The religious man has done the poorest possible service to his theme by talking about feeling or by pointing us to pleasure" (391).

Undoubtedly all higher values "yield a tribute of pleasure; but I cannot think tl is the most important fact regarding them" (392).

The impact of Hegelian intellectualism is, however, far more damaging t axiology than Ritschl's psychologism (393). Mackintosh doubts whether Hegel self took sides in the libertarian-determinist debate, but finds that his Englisl interpreters are unanimous in claiming that both Idealism and Naturalism den libertarian freedom, "and that, for all practical purposes - logical necessitat

)hysical compulsion. If we cannot repel this combined attack, it is idle to
ut values" (394).

ithetic values are distinctive, and depend upon personal perception, yet they
logous to moral and religious values. Concerning the former, "character is
:eme value of the universe" (395), and as to the latter, "salvation is offered
ighest of all religions as the highest of all values; in which every minor
ill find its due place, or for which - if need arises - many a minor value
joyfully surrendered in favour of that "one pearl of great price" "(396).
Mackintosh says many interesting things in <u>Values</u>, we take his own point
at had he analysed the concept of value <u>per se</u> instead of, or in addition to,
ing a quasi-descriptive study, the result might have been even more worth-

: upshot is that out of gratitude to God, and in the cause of the highest value,
istian and the Church must serve men and fulfil a prophetic role in society.
: seen already that Dr. Mackintosh was not afraid to make avowedly anti-paci-
ements, or to offer political judgements. He favoured capital punishment,
the dreadful possibility, which he recognised, of unrectifiable errors, on the
that "such naked and unrelieved punishment is a specially eloquent witness to
ibility and guilt. ... Were the citizen too trivial to be punished, he must sink
t of the mechanism of nature - too paltry to be ennobled by the love of man
e fear of God" (398). He upholds the sanctity of marriage, and, as we have
iewhere, contends that church and state have proper responsibilities towards
ier. He readily grants that there is much to be done at the practical level to
e world a better place, but, as so often, he adds a caution, significantly at
of one of his most intensely theological books:

> "It is better to have a bad creed and a good life than to have a good
> doctrine and a bad life. Happily, there is no need to choose one at
> the expense of the other.... Today we hear not indeed too much but
> disproportionately much about the evil of social injustice. Christ
> speaks to us of deeper needs; and yet the redeeming of social wrongs
> is a plain part of His programme.... If we fail to play our part, then
> perhaps humanitarian leaders who have no sure faith in Christ will
> serve Him better than we. But God forbid it! ... If we are humble and
> faithful and patient, then the day must be won, for God and for humani-
> ty, in the name of His holy Servant Jesus" (399).

CONCLUSION

emains to offer, after his own fashion, a tentative assessment of the thought Mackintosh. Among the many points which stand out, the following appear to cularly important and relevant.

ert Mackintosh anticipated the twentieth-century biblical theology movement ig to the heart of the scriptural witness. On the one hand, he appreciated the sults of the (in his day) new critical stance in biblical scholarship, but on the ind he never minimised or sought to undermine the over-all unity of the Vhilst some reacted to the higher criticism by retreating into an increasingly ed, uncritical orthodoxy, he passed new findings through his critical sieve ntained his balance throughout.

ckintosh does well to draw attention to the divide in Christendom over the ı of the priority of Gospel or Church - an issue which thus far would appear received less ecumenical attention than it deserves. The matter comes to a connection with the concept of episcopacy, but is basically a matter of diver- lerstandings of the grace of God. Further, his attitude towards creeds and ionalism is instructive, especially when, as at present, denominational ; are projected. Dr. Mackintosh's stress upon the fact of Christ's Lordship ole, Church, and creed seems to the present writer to be entirely appropriate. ame time it underlines the clamant need of a restatement of the doctrine of ' Spirit which shall do justice to his role as revealer of Christ, as prompter hristian's response, and as sustainer of the Church. The question of the relation to extra-churchly realms is raised by Mackintosh's glad recognition ings of Christ wherever they are to be found, and under whatsoever label vel.

doubt some of the things Mackintosh wrote concerning the Calvinism he left High Churchmanship he shunned are in the nature of "fighting talk". Calvinists licans will have their replies to make. We should remember, however, that osh was writing in <u>reaction</u> as far as Calvinism was concerned: he genuinely a legal bondage had been substituted for free grace in the circles in which he ı reared. We should remember too that we who now view his ecclesiological do so after a large quantity of ecumenical water has flowed under the bridge. ll, we should do well to take Mackintosh's <u>positive</u> point which amounts to an ing of the truth that Christ alone is Head of the Church and Saviour of men. l serve to make us as vigilant as he was against "another gospel" - whether ite from circles conservative or liberal, "high" or "low".

iough Dr. Mackintosh's analyses of some of the philosophical trends of his perceptive, the nature and spirit of much subsequent philosophy in the Anglo- orld make some of his remarks sound oddly dated. Whereas he can, for :, assume that the construction of a viable Christian philosophy is a real ity, the analysis of this very assumption itself constitutes a large part of ern of the contemporary philosopher of religion. Mackintosh never really took the measure of Russell or Moore, or weighed the possible impact upon th of the logical empiricism of the twenties. (In fairness, he was by no means al this.) Today, for instance, it would not be so easy to get away with the pronou ment that those who espouse what he called "half-Christianities" are imperfec enlightened men. A case would have to be made out which would take account (wide-ranging epistemological questions which proliferate on the Christian-hur frontier. On the other hand, he reads like a modern in his remarks upon natur theology, and in his conclusion upon the impossibility of producing a logical de stration of God's existence; and even Professor Flew would find himself in ag ment with Mackintosh upon the circularity which inevitably results when Chris wish to regard miracles as both signs to the believer and as evidence to the s(

Dr. Mackintosh's pre-Barthian case for dogmatic theology is refreshing t at a time when we are so frequently invited by some theologians to conduct the rites over that discipline as quickly as possible. The limits Mackintosh impos the subject, and the place he accords to reason are, however, salutary featur and reveal once again his sense of proportion. He kept his balance well, and w bowled over neither by any competing school of philosophy, whether evolutions or idealistic, nor yet by any brand of theology, whether liberal or orthodox. F never forgot that religion and faith are different in kind from philosophy and tl and therefore he was never guilty of a reduction of the former to the latter.

Finally, in his exposition of the heart of the Christian Gospel, Mackintosl emphasised the radical nature of sin at a time when some social gospel Christ were thinking over-optimistically in terms of removable blots and blemishes, when some orthodox theologians were making mournful noises over the fate of elect mankind at the hands of a capricious God. Again he trod a middle path, s to accord a due place to subjective and objective elements in atonement theory Above all, though convinced that personal salvation was to be found in Christ s he was never individualistic about it. For him the Christian life is a life of fel ship. In this sense the Church is necessary, and neccessarily committed to be about its Lord's business in the world.

We are thus left with a thinker who in his day, and after a personally dem spiritual quest, walked a middle road in theology, and whose grasp of the cent issues of the faith was sure. As far as possible we have allowed him to speak himself, and we trust we have not misrepresented him. He deserves a hearing may be that the balanced and judicious do not hit the headlines so readily as th blamboyant and sensational. It would be a pity if this fact, coupled with the fac theology's proneness to fashions were to deprive the contemporary Church of] peculiarly relevant insights. Already the Barthian sun is somewhat dimmed, a many are unpersuaded either that God is dead, or that process thought will pr theology's panacaea. It is not impossible, therefore, that the general position Robert Mackintosh, a position we might sum up as moderate-critical-evangeli may come to be reiterated. If this were to happen - albeit in a context in some far removed from his own - it would be a pity if he were to go unacknowledged

APPENDIX A

THE WORKS OF DR. MACKINTOSH

ks
—

and the Jewish Law, London: Hodder & Stoughton, 1886.
Towards a New Theology, Glasgow: Maclehose 1889. (This volume includes CF and IRRS)
omte to Benjamin Kidd, London: Macmillan 1899.
Primer of Apologetics, London: Elliot Stock 1900; second revised ed., London: A. Melrose 1904.
nd Hegelianism, Edinburgh: T. & T. Clark 1903.
al Rainy, London: Melrose 1907.
onians and Corinthians (in the Westminster New Testament series), London: lrose 1909.
in Ethics, London: T.C. and E.C. Jack, 1909.
inity and Sin, London: Duckworth 1913.
t Ritschl and His School, London: Chapman & Hall 1915.
Theories of Atonement, London: Hodder & Stoughton 1920.
London: Independent Press 1928.
entral Things, London: Independent Press 1932.

presentative Articles, Contributions and Reviews

act of the Atonement," ET, vol. 14, 1902-3, pp. 344-350.
hrist Fulfilled the Prophecies," in Is Christianity True? - a series of tures delivered in the Central Hall, Manchester, 1904, pp. 283-304.
wn of Messianic Consciousness," ET, vol. 16, 1904-5, pp. 157-8, 211-15, -70.
ion and the Doctrine of Sin," in Theological Essays, ed. A.S. Peake (the ugural Lectures of the Faculty of Theology, Manchester), 1905.
s (N.B. those on "Call", "Fulfilment", "Historical", and "Universalism") in)ictionary of Christ and the Gospels, ed. J. Hastings, vol. I 1906; vol. II 8.
iti-Christ of II Thessalonians," Exp, 7th ser. vol. 2, 1906, pp. 427-432.
sor Gwatkin on Revelation," ET, vol. 18, 1906-7, pp. 221-3.
ige Problems at Corinth," Exp, 7th ser. vol. 4, 1907, pp. 349-363.
h and the Tragedy of St. Paul", Exp, 7th ser. vol. 6, 1908, pp. 77-83.
ief Visit to Corinth," Exp, 7th ser. vol. 6, 1908, pp. 226-234.
ur Perplexing Chapters (2 Cor. x-xiii)," Exp, 7th ser. vol. 6, 1908, 336-344.
Philosophy and Christian Doctrine," PICC (3), 1908, pp. 76-84.

Articles on Christians (Names Applied To), Monolatry and Henotheism in Enc Religion and Ethics, ed. J. Hastings, 1908 ff.

Articles on Anthropomorphism, Apologetics, Apotheosis, Dogma, Theism an logy in Encyc. Brit. 11th edn., 1910-11.

"The Roots of St. Paul's Doctrine of Sin," Exp, 8th ser. vol. 5, 1913, pp. 44

"The Life Story of Albrecht Ritschl," Exp, 8th ser. vol. 8, 1914, pp. 550-56

"Galatians," in Peake's Commentary on the Bible, ed. A.S. Peake, 1919.

"Herbert Spencer: A Centenary Estimate," HR, July 1920, pp. 289-305.

"The Contribution of British Congregationalism to Religious Thought," PICC 1920, pp. 119-123.

"The Beatitudes," ET, vol. 32, 1920-21, pp. 519-520.

"Christian Unity and Church Union," HR, Jan. 1921, pp. 32-44.

"Nonconformity in the Universities: Manchester," CQ, vol. 2, 1924, pp. 90-!

"Dr. Whyte as I Remember Him," CQ, vol. 2, 1924, pp. 196-205.

"The Theology of COPEC," HJ, vol. 23, 1924-5, pp. 85-100.

"Recent Thought on the Doctrine of the Atonement," ET, vol. 37, 1925-6, pp. 203.

"Thomas Henry Huxley," HR, Oct. 1925, pp. 489-506.

"Theological Aphorisms," CQ, vol. 5, 1927, pp. 51-56.

"The Religion of the 'Shorter Catechism'," HR, Jan. 1927, pp. 16-25.

Review of F.R. Tennant's Philosophical Theology, vol. I, CQ, vol. 6, 1928, pp. 493-4.

Art. on Apologetics, Encyc.Brit. 14th ed., 1929.

Review of F.R. Tennant's Philosophical Theology, vol. II, CQ, vol. 8, 1930, pp. 374-7.

"The Living Church: The Expression of Its Life: Its Sacraments," PICC (5), pp. 136-143.

"My Experiments in Authorship," CQ, vol. 9, 1931, pp. 279-288.

"The Genius of Congregationalism," in Essays Congregational and Catholic, A. Peel, 1931, pp. 103-125.

Review of K.E. Kirk's The Vision of God, CQ, vol. 9, 1931, pp. 357-9.

Discussion of a paper by R.S. Franks on "The Person of Christ," CQ, vol. 1 1932, pp. 38-42.

"Church Union - Hopes and Cautions," CQ, vol. 11, 1933, pp. 32-44.

APPENDIX B

SOME FURTHER WORDS OF DR. ROBERT MACKINTOSH

ere follows a selection of passages designed to illustrate further not only Dr. osh's attitude towards a variety of issues, but also his crisp, and sometimes manner of expressing his views.

e Wordly Wisdom

ty public man's success may be regarded as the sum of different factors. If is due to his merit, the rest is due to the blunders committed by his critics ls" (400).

ersons, who herd in corners with those who share their prejudices, are apt he whisperings of a coterie for the verdict of 'the civilised world,' or even lmighty" (401).

e verdicts on others

tler fears profoundly that there must be a just God who will punish us. Kant with tolerable strength of conviction, that there may be a just God who will us" (402).

ubtless the archdeacon (i.e. Paley) knew nothing of the German professor nt) and would have cared nothing for him however well he had known him"

Hegel: "We never feel the beat of a heart in his writings - only the pulse of A manual of Differential Calculus will appear a warm and sentimental when compared with the merciless pages in which Hegel anatomises the man or the nature of the Blessed God. Nothing that he has said will, by the of his saying it, make anyone the braver for reading it or the better for ering it. The philosopher has almost if not altogether eaten out the 04).

eod "Campbell brushes aside original sin because 'usually present to the a dogma and not as a consciousness.' This incidental verdict, gentle and e a tap from a lion's paw, suggests a whole apparatus of criticism and con- n" (405).

m a review of F.J. Sheen, Religion without God: "When the author has to spell the names of those he attacks, and to bring his statements of histori-

cal fact into some sort of relation with accuracy, then it will be time for the ?
testant reader to enquire whether Dr. Sheen's theories offer a contribution to
the common Christian stock. Not that the prospect appears bright" (406).

(vi) "In a perfectly friendly notice of my book Mr. Mozley described me as a
lance' - hardly to my contentment. Evangelical Christians hate legalism, yet
always to be 'not without law to God, but under law to Christ.' Still, that does
exactly imply that we are under law to the Ecumenical Councils; and the kind]
of Anglo-Catholics may find the distinction subtle" (407).

(c) On the Bible

"Why will men idolise the Book, or quarrel over the Book? God has left blots
Book that we may not stop short at it, or make of it an idol, but may apprehe:
true use - that it testifies to us of Christ" (408).

(d) On the contortions of Confessional theology

"Hence the marvellous statement - perhaps the most marvellous in the whole
fession - that Scripture is "not manifold." Doubtless, to the dogmatist, peeri
about everywhere for proof texts, the differences have no meaning. Hill, vall
and plain, cliff and waterfall, are nothing to the man with the muck rake. Ass
ly, what one sees depends on the observer even more than on the object. But
Confessional use of proof-texts is even more precious and beautiful than the (
fessional affirmations about them.... Difficult questions on the doctrine of P:
dence are settled by the story of David and the men of Keilah. Finally - and I
specially recommend this to the admirers of the Establishment principle - th
proof that the civil magistrate may lawfully summon religious synods is founc
the fact that Herod consulted the chief priests in order to plot more successfu
how to murder the infant Jesus. Comment on these citations could be nothing
feeble anti-climax. Let us treasure them up in our hearts" (409).

(e) On the failure of the Church to take theological reconstruction seriously
---

Honest theological reconstruction "ought to have been the Church's recognised
for at least a century past. Instead of which, we have been engaged in devoutl
thanking God that we, at least, were not like other men, troubled with doubts
astray from the safe pastures of the seventeenth century - or even as those G
mans" (410).

sential features of Christianity are summed up in the revelation of God as
haracter, not in His revelation as infinite power. God's omnipotence is
osed; but any manifestation of God which proceeds on the ground of mere
ence is disparate from our very nature. When the Scotist doctrine of moral
the Calvinistic doctrine of predestination, or the forensic doctrine of the
ent, reduces the manifestation of God to an inscrutable force, however great
mg, it denies Christ. We know God as the good, and as the source of good-
lough the processes by which God works are inherently mysterious. We may
ble to think together God's moral purpose with His almighty power. No
God reveals Himself to us as a moral and gracious purpose; we have to
His revelation as He is pleased to give it; and our consciences do not fail to
witness. For, while other things are matters of curiosity, moral things
our true selves; God's grace is our life.

, in Christ, the character of God comes to meet us with forgiveness for our
ause God is God and Father, and with the pledge of perfect victory over evil
vho deny themselves and follow Christ. If we commit ourselves to His power,
ever fail us.

1 God as our Father, and in Christ as the Saviour of the world, is Christian
'hatever obscures this is leaven of the Scribes and Pharisees" (411).

NOTES

5, p. 4.
…ve much of the material in the following two paragraphs to Memorials of the
…. C.C. Mackintosh, D.D. of Tain and Dunoon, Edited with a Sketch of the
…igious History of the Northern Highlands of Scotland by the Rev. William
…lor, M.A., Stirling. Edinburgh, 1870.
… her life see J. Anderson, Ladies of the Covenant, Edinburgh, 1862.
…tches of Charles Calder and Angus McIntosh may be found in J. Kennedy,
… Days of the Fathers in Ross-shire, 2nd edn. Edinburgh 1861, pp. 52-6
… 72-5 respectively. Old St. Duthus Church, Tain, contains a memorial
…dow inscribed: "'Blessed are the dead who die in the Lord'. In loving
mory of Angus Mackintosh and his son Charles Calder Mackintosh, ministers
Tain 1789, 1854". Tain Museum houses some baby clothes emroidered by
…rles's widow, Robert's mother. Charles was Clerk of the Tain presbytery
…he time of the Disruption, and of all the local ministers one only, the ailing
…gh Ross of Fearn, did not "come out". For this and further details of local
…lesiastical history see R.W. Munro and Jean Munro, Tain Through the
…turies, Tain Town Council 1966, chap. 10.
… T. Brown, Annals of the Disruption, Edinburgh, 1893, p. 810.
…wards the end of his life he advanced the view that the establishment principle
…d not be an obstacle to union with those who did not hold it. For a statement
…he establishment principle as held by the Free Church of Scotland cf. the
…stminster Confession of Faith (approved by Parliament on 20th June 1648)
…p. XXIII, especially section III: 'The civil magistrate ... hath authority,
… it is his duty, to take order, that unity and peace be preserved in the
…rch, that the truth of God be kept pure and entire, that all blasphemies
… heresies be suppressed, all corruptions and abuses in worship and disci-
…e prevented or reformed, and all ordinances of God duly settled, administer-
… and observed. For the better effecting whereof, he hath power to call
…ods, to be present at them, and to provide that whatsoever is transacted in
…m be according to the mind of God." Similar statements may be found in the
…ldensian Confession (1532), Melanchthon's Saxon Confession (1551), the
…ttish Confession (1560), J.H. Bullinger's Second Helvetic Confession (1566),
… By an Act of the Free Church Assembly (Act xii, 1846) it was determined
…t the confessional statements concerning the civil magistrate should be
…lerstood as requiring that person to lend moral support and encouragement
…he officer of the Church, and as forbidding intolerant and pursecutory atti-
…es and measures. The following is an assessment of the situation at the
…ruption of 1843: "The Free Church separated from the Established Church
…Scotland in the year 1843; not because she ceased to hold the duty of the
…il Magistrate as set forth in her Confession of Faith; but on account of the
…il Magistrate's intrusion into the spiritual jurisdiction of the Church. Dr.
…almers declared on the day of the Disruption: "We have left to-day a vitiated
…:ablishment, we would return tomorrow to a purified one; and we are not

Voluntaries."" See History of the Free Presbyterian Church (1893-1970) compiled by a Synod Committee, F.P. Publications, 1975, p. 20.
7) Memorials, p. 53. For further contemporary testimony to the effects of 1840 revival see e.g. T. Brown, Annals of the Disruption; with Extracts the Narratives of Ministers who left the Scottish Establishment in 1843, : burgh, 1893, chap. II.
8) Quoted in T. Brown, Annals of the Disruption, pp. 77-78.
9) Congregations of the Free Church of Scotland continue to this day in Tain Dunoon. See Free Church of Scotland Year Book, Edinburgh, 1972, pp. ɛ and 10.
10) V, p. 86 n. For a contrary testimony see e.g. Taylor's preface to the Memorials of the Rev. C.C. Mackintosh, pp. 9-10: "Never assuredly dic music more truly express a sentiment of the heart than do these wild mel with their prolonged and swelling cadences, so plaintive and meditative, when heard in the great open-air congregations, so sublime, represent tl very tone and character of the religion of the district."
11) R. Mackintosh, "Dr. Whyte as I remember him," CQ, vol. 2, 1924, p. :
12) PR, pp. 8-9.
13) Ibid., p. 9.
14) Ibid., pp. 9-10.
15) Ibid., p. 3 n.
16) Eneas Mackintosh (born 1855) studied at Glasgow University and became minister of the Presbyterian Church in England. He was assistant in Gibɪ (1883-4) and then, after training at Dunedin Theological College, he was ordained in New Zealand in 1885. Eventually, after a period of ill health, having returned to Britain, he was inducted to the charge at Holybourne c 13th June 1894. There he remained until his death on 10th February 1924 there he was buried. Mr. A.G. Esslemont of the United Reformed Churc ry Society and Dr. J.C. O'Neill of Cambridge kindly supplied this inform
17) Mackintosh won the following prizes: 1872-73, 7th prize Junior Greek, 4ɩ Junior Latin; 1873-74, Senior Latin class: Cowan Gold Medal, prize for Excellence and two prizes for examinations on prescribed books; 1874-7! 4th prize Junior Logic; 1875-76, 2nd prize Junior Moral Philosophy; 187 5th prize Natural Philosophy, and 1st prize Higher Metaphysics. He also a Coulter Prize for the best Latin essay on "The True Relation of the Sta Education." I am indebted to Mr. Neil Robertson of the University of Gla for supplying me with lists of Mackintosh's subjects, Professors and priː Glasgow.
18) CQ, vol. 9, 1931, p. 285.
19) "Dr. Whyte as I Remember Him," CQ, vol. 2, 1924, p. 200.
20) Ibid., p. 204.
21) Ibid., pp. 197-8.
22) PR, pp. 74-75. During his college days the Theological Society asked Ma to support "education" in a debate on the motion "Is life better viewed as tion than as probation?" Whilst reading up Erskine of Linlathen in prepar for his speech he became convinced that belief in eternal punishment mus See op.cit. pp. 73-74.

ey were: Rev. Robert Rainy, D.D., Principal and Professor of Church
tory; Rev. James Macgregor, D.D., Professor of Systematic Theology;
r. A.B. Davidson, D.D., Litt. D., LL.D., Professor of Old Testament;
r. John Duns, Professor of Natural Science; Rev. George Smeaton, D.D.,
ofessor of New Testament; Rev. W.G. Blaikie, D.D., LL.D., Professor
Apologetics, Christian Ethics, and Practical Theology; and the teacher of
cution, Dr. Anderson Moxey. I am indebted to Erma R. Leslie of New
lege for this list of teachers, and for other information concerning
ckintosh's period at the College.
y Experiments in Authorship," CQ, vol. 9, 1931, p. 279.
l., p. 279.
l., p. 280.
l., p. 281.
, p. 75.
neral oration, p. 12.
S, p. 107.
, pp. 67-68. The Declaratory Act was passed in 1892, and in 1893 the Free
esbyterian Church was constituted in protest. This Church claims to stand
the true Disruption succession. So, for that matter, does the continuing
ee Church of Scotland, whose forebears refused to join the majority of their
thren who, on 31st October, 1900, united with the United Presbyterian
rch (a body which maintained the voluntary principle in the line of one of
forebears, the Relief Church) to form the United Free Church of Scotland.
ckintosh could not approve the attitude of the Free Church minority in 1900,
because they claimed rights in the law courts, but because their case
sted on the ground that a free, Christian church has no right to revise its
ed. At the same time, he felt that the majority could have been more
erously disposed towards them. (See PR, pp. 99-101). The majority of
U.F. Church united with the Established Church in 1929, though a remnant
F. Church continues. As recently as 1968 the seventy-fifth anniversary of
F.P. Church occasioned exchanges between themselves and the Free Church
to which of the two is truly the continuing Disruption Church. For this see
e Free Presbyterian Magazine, August, 1968, and The Monthly Record of
Free Church of Scotland, September, 1968. See also, D. Maclean, Aspects
Scottish Church History, Edinburgh, 1927, Lecture IV; G.N.M. Collins,
e Heritage of our Fathers, Edinburgh, 1974; History of the Free Presbyterian
urch of Scotland, 1893-1970, compiled by a Synod Committee, F.P. Publi-
ions, 1975; J. Colquhoun, "The Present Position and Prospects of the Re-
med Church in Scotland," in Papers Commemorating the Quarter-Centenary
the Scottish Reformation, F.P. Publications, 1960, pp. 62-68. Most of the
egoing are unashamedly partisan.
ese were published (slightly amended) in CQ, vol. 5, 1927, prefaced inter
a by the remark here quoted.
y Experiments in Authorship," CQ, vol. 9, 1931, p. 281.
ese were published in one volume, with ETANT in 1899.
RS, pp. 6-8.
l., p. 10.

37) IRRS, p. 13.
38) Ibid., p. 16.
39) Ibid., pp. 27-28.
40) Ibid., p. 40.
41) OWCF, pp. 63-64.
42) IRRS, p. 37.
43) See "My Experiments in Authorship," CQ, vol. 9, 1931, p. 282.
44) "A New Plea for Evangelism," ET, vol. 22, 1910-11, p. 522.
45) "My Experiments in Authorship," CQ, vol. 9, 1931, p. 282.
46) Ibid., p. 283.
47) Ibid.
48) Ibid.
49) Quoted by John S. Richards in "Death of Dr. Mackintosh," BW, 16th Feb 1933.
50) I am indebted to the Rev. A.L. MacArthur for putting me in touch with M R.J. Watson, Hon. Librarian of the Presbyterian Historical Society of E1 He in turn kindly obtained the information relating to Mackintosh's servi Withington from the then minister of the Presbyterian church there, the Rev. J.V. Henderson.
51) IRRS, p. 36.
52) "The Genius of Congregationalism," in Essays Congregational and Catho A. Peel, 1931, p. 105.
53) "My Experiments in Authorship," p. 287.
54) FPA, pp. 3-4. The words "probably even" in the first line of the quotatic somewhat quaintly on the modern ear.
55) This church was formed in 1805 or 1806. Mackintosh's successor but one the pastorate (1901-1907) was John Murphy, M.A., B.D., who, in 1930 succeeded him at Lancashire Independent College. See H. Escott, A Hist of Scottish Congregationalism, Glasgow, 1960, p. 347. For J. Murphy (1950) See CYB, 1950, p. 520.
56) I am most grateful to the Rev. Thomas Mearns, M.A., the present mini at Dumfries for supplying copies of the minutes and letters here reprodu
57) Dr. D.W. Simon (1830-1909) went from Spring Hill College, Birminghan Edinburgh, to become Principal and Professor of Systematic Theology th in 1884. He subsequently became Principal of Airedale College. See F.J Powicke, David Worthington Simon, 1912, and CYB 1910, p. 189. For th history of the Yorkshire Congregational academies/colleges, see K.W. \ worth, Yorkshire United Independent College, 1954.
58) PR, p. 75.
59) Ibid., p. 53.
60) I owe this reference to Mr. Griffiths to Dr. J.W. Batty, the present sec of Withington church, who supplied much helpful information concerning fellowship.
61) A.J. Grieve in Mackintosh's obituary notice, CYB, 1934, p. 269.
62) So Grieve, "Funeral Oration," p. 10. For Scott (1831-1919), Principal, 1902, see CYB, 1920, pp. 112-113; Adeney (1849-1920), Principal, 190! see CYB, 1921, p. 102; Bennett (1855-1920), Principal, 1913-1920 see (

!1, p. 103; Grieve (1874-1952), Principal, 1922-1943, see CYB, 1953, 508-9, and C.E. Surman (Grieve's son-inlaw), <u>Alexander James Grieve</u>, nchester, 1953.
ıas not proved possible to trace a copy of the eulogy.
N.S. vol. 10, 1901, pp. 267-269.
Ball, op.cit., p. 268.
1., p. 269.
connection with his penultimate book, V, 1928, Mackintosh wrote, "who was to speak the "last word" upon any great theme?" See "My Experiments in horship," CQ, vol. 9, 1931, p. 288.
ı. Richards, BW, 16.2.33.
y Experiments in Authorship," CQ, vol. 9, 1931, pp. 283-4.
J. Grieve, "Funeral Oration," p. 13.
ı. Richards, "Death of Dr. Mackintosh," BW, 16.2.33.
G. Theobald, "Mainly Reminiscent," Lancashire College Old Students' sociation Magazine, October 1933.
om a letter to the author. I have been greatly helped by a numer of Dr. ckintosh's surviving students who have responded to my request for informa-ı, reminiscences, etc.
ı letter to the author.
, vol. 16, 1904-5, p. 85.
e series was "The World's Epoch-Makers," edited by Oliphant Smeaton.
y Experiments in Authorship," CQ, vol. 9, 1931, p. 287. Mackintosh comnts, "Perhaps editors have to abound in civilities of that order."
1., pp. 287-8.
1., p. 286.
5. Peake (1865-1929) was a Primitive Methodist layman. A teacher first at ford and subsequently at Hartley Primitive Methodist College, Manchester, became the first Rylands Professor of Biblical Criticism and Exegesis at nchester University. For a recent study see John T. Wilkinson, <u>Arthur nuel Peake</u>, 1971.
.ppeared in ET, vol. 14, 1902-3, pp. 344-350.
PICC (3), 1908, pp. 76-84.
1., p. 124. Dr. Duff (1845-1934) was appointed from McGill to Airedale .lege in 1878 to teach Old Testament and Mathematics. From 1888 to 1958 College, amalgamated with Rotherham College, continued as Yorkshire ted Independent College. A further amalgamation then occurred, this time h Mackintosh's own College, Lancashire.
r representative titles see Appendix A (ii) above.
y Experiments in Authorship," CQ, vol. 9, 1931, pp. 286-7.
W. Gordon Robinson, <u>A History of the Lancashire Congregational Union</u>, !6-1956, Manchester, 1955, p. 73.
onconformity in the Universities, V. Manchester," CQ, vol. 2, 1924, pp. -95.
nuel Alexander (1859-1938) was Professor of Philosophy at Manchester m 1893-1924.
<u>Theological Essays</u>, ed. A.S. Peake, Manchester, 1905, being the Inaugural ctures of the Faculty of Theology, Manchester.

90) My search for a copy of this address has not been successful. The Regis of the University and the Tutor to the Faculty of Theology are to be thank their efforts in this matter.
91) "My Experiments in Authorship," CQ, vol. 9, 1931, p. 287.
92) See ET, vol. 26, 1914-15, p. 309.
93) See Garvie's review of ARS in HJ, vol. 13, 1914-15, pp. 915-918.
94) See above, p. 24.
95) See his review in HJ, vol. 20, 1921-2, pp. 391-5.
96) Later to become Principal of Mansfield College, Oxford. The late Dr. M kindly favoured me with his memories of the period. See also his The Bc the Puppets, 1957, pp. 58-60.
97) Year Book of the Lancashire Congregational Union, 1918. The late Rev. Figures, M.A., sometime Moderator of the N.W. Province of the Congr nal Church in England and Wales, and Secretary of the Lancashire Union supplied this extract. Cf. W. Gordon Robinson, op.cit., p. 94.
98) Quoted by C.E. Surman, Alexander James Grieve, Manchester, 1953, p cf. ibid., p. 95.
99) I.e. Conference on Christian Politics, Economics and Citizenship, held Birmingham, April 5th-12th, 1924.
100) "Recent Thought on the Doctrine of the Atonement," ET, vol. 37, 1925-6 p. 203.
101) COPEC Commission Reports, 1924, pp. 85-86.
102) "The Theology of COPEC," HJ, vol. 23, 1924-5, p. 89.
103) Ibid., p. 91.
104) Ibid., p. 97.
105) Ibid., p. 100.
106) Op.cit., p. 15.
107) Anonymous obituary, BW, 16th February, 1933.
108) A.J. Grieve, "Funeral Oration," p. 11.
109) G. Phillips, "Dr. Mackintosh," The Congregational Monthly, Lancashire March 1933, p. xi. Mr. Phillips (1893-1967) subsequently became a Pro at Lancashire College. For his Biography see CYB 1968-69, p. 440.
110) See Appendix A (ii) for a selection of these.
111) "My Experiments in Authorship," CQ, vol. 9, 1931, p. 286.
112) ET, vol. 40, 1928-9, p. 195.
113) CQ, vol. 7, 1929, p. 113.
114) "My Experiments in Authorship," p. 288.
115) V, p. 121.
116) SCT, p. 2.
117) Report, "Retirement of Dr. Mackintosh," The Manchester Guardian, Jur 1930.
118) The details in this paragraph are culled from Dr. Grieve's obituary notic CYB, 1934, p. 269.
119) The Rev. C.L. Wilson in a letter to the author.
120) The Rev. J.M. Calder in a letter to the author.
121) The Rev. C.E. Surman in a letter to the author.
122) G. Phillips, "Dr. Mackintosh," The Congregational Monthly, Mancheste edition, March 1933, p. xi.

I. Grieve, "Funeral Oration," pp. 12,13,14,15.
p. 99.
L, App. C, pp. 245-6.
S, p. 202.
ie Fact of the Atonement," ET, vol. 14, 1902-3, p. 350.
ie Living Church: The Expression of its Life. Its Sacraments," PICC (5),
0, p. 142.
CF, p. 6; and passim for the views here summarised.
i., p. 32.
ANT, p. 345.
CF, p. 12.
ANT, p. 348.
i., p. 400.
S, p. 5.
ANT, p. 457.
i., p. 433.
i., p. 434.
i., p. 468.
CF, p. 27.
i.
i., p. 29.
A, p. 106.
cussion of R.S. Franks's paper, "The Person of Christ in the Light of
dern Scholarship," CQ, vol 10, 1932, p. 39.
, pp. 68-9.
CF, p. 60.
, p. 96. His Free Church brethren at the time of the Declaratory Act who
)osed the Act made a mistake that the Disruption fathers would never have
de. "Scripture was irreformable to them, but nothing else was." Ibid.
:C (4), New York, 1920, p. 121.
iurch Union - Hopes and Cautions," CQ, vol. 11, 1933, p. 453.
ǝ most recent Declaration is that of 1967.
ie Genius of Congregationalism," in Essays Congregational and Catholic,
A. Peel, 1931, p. 122.
i., p. 107.
i., pp. 106-7.
iristian Unity and Church Union," HR, Jan. 1921, p. 33.
)nconformity in the Universities: V, Manchester," CQ, vol. 2, 1924, p. 96.
iurch Union - Hopes and Cautions," CQ, vol. 11, 1933, p. 452. It was
: to latter-day Congregationalists to work out the idea of a churchly body
ch is yet congregational, rather than episcopalian or consistorial in
iracter.
ie Genius of Congregationalism," op.cit., p. 125.
L, p. 190.
ANT, pp. 350-351.
CF, p. 47.
i., p. 51.

162) <u>OWCF</u>, p. 55.
163) <u>ETANT</u>, pp. 244-5, and cf. <u>FPA</u>, pp. 71-4.
164) <u>ETANT</u>, p. 391.
165) <u>Ibid.</u>, p. 392.
166) "The Living Church: The Expression of its Life. Its Sacraments," <u>PICC</u> 1930, p. 140.
167) <u>OWCF</u>, p. 7.
168) <u>ETANT</u>, p. 454.
169) <u>OWCF</u>, p. 9. Elsewhere, on the same point, he remarks, "No doubt ... illogical English temperament is able to combine a spiritual faith with a stitious doctrine better than most men could do. But truth is truth." <u>IRRS</u> p. 34.
170) "The Living Church ... Its Sacraments," <u>PICC</u> (5) 1930, p. 142.
171) <u>IRRS</u>, p. 33.
172) <u>Ibid.</u>, p. 34.
173) <u>Ibid.</u>, p. 35.
174) <u>Op.cit.</u>, pp. 85,86.
175) "The Theology of COPEC," <u>HJ</u> vol. 23, 1924-5, p. 89.
176) <u>Op.cit.</u>, pp. 71,74.
177) <u>Ibid.</u>, p. 91.
178) <u>CAS</u>, p. 105.
179) <u>HTA</u>, p. 222.
180) "The Living Church ... Its Sacraments," <u>PICC</u> (5) 1930, p. 140.
181) <u>IRRS</u>, p. 8.
182) <u>Ibid.</u>
183) For which see "The Living Church ... Its Sacraments," pp. 136-140.
184) <u>Ibid.</u>, p. 139.
185) <u>Ibid.</u>
186) <u>IRRS</u>, p. 28.
187) <u>Ibid.</u>
188) <u>Ibid.</u>
189) <u>Op.cit.</u>, p. 104.
190) "The Living Church ... Its Sacraments," p. 140.
191) <u>Ibid.</u>, p. 141.
192) <u>Ibid.</u>, p. 138.
193) <u>Ibid.</u>
194) "Recent Thought on the Doctrine of the Atonement," <u>ET</u> vol. 37, 1925-6,
195) "The Living Church ... Its Sacraments," p. 140.
196) <u>Ibid.</u>
197) <u>Ibid.</u>, p. 141.
198) <u>Ibid.</u>
199) <u>Ibid.</u>, p. 143.
200) Cf. the following from the Report of the Liturgical Group of the Congrega Union of England and Wales, November, 1965, pp. 12-13: "The early Cor gationalists held that only a minister in office as pastor of the church cou preside at the Lord's Supper. "Where there are no teaching Officers, nor administer the Seals, nor can the Church authorise any so to do." (Savoy

ion, Platform of Polity, XVI). When Isaac Watts became pastor of Mark
ie Meeting in 1702 the church had not had the Lord's Supper for nearly a
r (since the resignation of his predecessor) although there were three re-
:d ministers who were members of the church. ... In later years it was
erally accepted that any ordained minister might be invited by a church to
ainister the sacrament. Then towards the end of the nineteenth century ...
ame to be more loosely held that any church member might preside, even
he minister was present. ... There appears to be no reference to 'lay
ebration' in Congregationalism older than 100 years ago."
ie Genius of Congregationalism," <u>Essays Congregational and Catholic</u>, ed.
Peel, 1931, p. 123.
ie Living Church ... Its Sacraments," p. 143.
<u>I.</u>
<u>IS</u>, p. 36. He wrote this <u>before</u> he became a Congregationalist.
essalonians and Corinthians in "The Westminster New Testament," ed. A.E.
vie, 1909, p. 86.
urch Union - Hopes and Cautions," <u>CQ</u>, vol. 11, 1933, p. 450.
<u>l.</u> p. 455.
<u>A</u>, p. 221.
ie contribution of British Congregationalism to religious thought: our present
ength and weakness in that field," <u>PICC</u> (4), 1920, p. 121.
<u>CF</u>, pp. 16-17.
iristian Unity and Church Union," <u>HR</u>, Jan. 1921, p. 38.
<u>l.</u>, p. 39.
<u>l.</u>, p. 40.
<u>l.</u>, p. 41-2.
<u>l.</u>, p. 43.
, p. 41. The majority of Free Churchmen turned voluntarist in 1900. The
tinuing Free Church, and also the Free Presbyterian Church (of the 1893
ession) still uphold the establishment principle.
<u>l.</u>, p. 20.
<u>l.</u>, p. 21.
<u>l.</u>, p. 22.
<u>l.</u>, p. 23.
<u>CF</u>, pp. 21-22.
, p. 108.
<u>CF</u>, p. 24.
<u>I.</u>
<u>IS</u>, p. 32.
iristian Unity and Church Union," <u>HR</u>, Jan. 1921, p. 34.
<u>l.</u>, p. 35.
<u>IS</u>, p. 32.
, p. 50.
<u>H</u>, p. 257.
<u>l.</u>, pp. 257-8.
<u>A</u>, pp. 192-3.
<u>ANT</u>, p. 145.

234) CBK, chap. XI.
235) ARS, e.g. pp. 158, 165, 170.
236) "Theism," Encyc. Brit. 11th ed., 1910-11, vol. 26, p. 747.
237) Ibid., p. 753.
238) Ibid.
239) Ibid.
240) Ibid.
241) CBK, chap. VII.
242) Ibid., pp. 78-9.
243) Ibid., p. 85.
244) Ibid., chaps. I-VI.
245) Ibid., p. 21.
246) Ibid., p. 22.
247) Ibid., p. 29.
248) Ibid., p. 8.
249) Ibid., p. 281.
250) "Recent Philosophy and Christian Doctrine," PICC (3), 1908, pp. 81-82. one wishes that Mackintosh had written a further paper, under the same t twenty years later - after the initial impact of logical empiricism!
251) "Theism," op. cit., p. 747.
252) Ibid., p. 748.
253) Mackintosh is, of course, a child of his time in not questioning the role o philosopher as adumbrator of a speculative system.
254) "Theism," op. cit., p. 748.
255) Ibid., p. 749.
256) Ibid.
257) Ibid., p. 750.
258) See HAH, pp. 276-291.
259) Ibid., p. 277.
260) Ibid., p. 287.
261) Ibid., p. 290.
262) Ibid.
263) Ibid., p. 291.
264) ETANT, p. 366.
265) "Recent Philosophy and Christian Doctrine," PICC (3), 1908, p. 83.
266) FPA, p. 33.
267) Mackintosh carefully discusses the term "natural theology" and related te in his article "Theism," op. cit., pp. 744-745. We follow this article for potted history of the subject.
268) "Theism," op. cit., p. 746.
269) Ibid., p. 750.
270) Albeit over twenty years after Hume had demolished it!
271) "Theism," op. cit., p. 748.
272) Ibid., p. 753.
273) Ibid., p. 755.
274) Ibid., p. 748. Mackintosh also notes (p. 752) the earlier form of the mor argument (here closely linked with the design argument) which appears

Raymond of Sabunde: if human life is not to be "vain" there must be a God to reward and punish.
theism," op.cit., p. 755.
I., p. 757.
ANT, pp. 365-6. Would that Mackintosh, instead of contenting himself with his ad hominem appeal had argued the case with e.g. Robert Flint, who would by no means have agreed with him.
I., p. 366.
I.
A, pp. 38-39.
ANT, p. 359.
I., p. 380.
A, p. 11, and cf. pp. 9-11.
ANT, pp. 370-371.
"Professor Gwatkin on Revelation," ET, vol. 18, 1906-7, p. 223.
ANT, p. 372.
CAS, pp. 90-91.
"Professor Gwatkin on Revelation," op.cit., p. 223.
ANT, p. 336. If we were to understand Mackintosh (anachronistically, of course) to be drawing attention to the existential nature of Christian knowledge, we should probably not be far wide of the mark.
3, pp. 252-3.
I., p. 255.
Review of F.R. Tennant's Philosophical Theology, vol. II, CQ, vol. 8, 1930, p. 375.
ANT, p. 389.
"Recent Philosophy and Christian Doctrine," PICC (3), 1908, p. 84. Cf. CAS 155: "We have to steer a careful course between naturalistic philosophies, which never permit ethics to come into being, and pantheising philosophies of the Absolute, which claim to transcend the contrast between right and wrong."
"Theological Aphorisms," CQ, vol. 5, 1927, p. 57.
CF, p. 58.
"Theology," Encyc.Brit. 11th ed., 1910-11, vol. 26, p. 773.
ANT, p. 408.
I., pp. 39-40.
"Theological Aphorisms," op.cit., p. 52.
"The Theology of COPEC," HJ, vol. 23, 1924-5, p. 91.
ANT, p. 382.
I., p. 381.
"Theological Aphorisms," op.cit., p. 56.
A, p. 13.
I.
CF, p. 44.
I. A prophecy which was to come true in the writings of e.g. Otto, Oman, John Baillie. A revival of interest in religious (i.e. not necessarily Christian) experience appears to be under way in the present post-Barthian, more 'open-ended' period.

309) FPA, p. 84.
310) ETANT, p. 100.
311) Ibid., p. 101.
312) Ibid., p. 384. Even the Westminster divines are charged with caring mo their system than for historicity. Ibid., p. 353.
313) "Apologetics," Encyc.Brit. 11th ed., 1910-11, p. 192.
314) ETANT, p. 95.
315) Ibid., p. 405.
316) Ibid., p. 29.
317) Ibid., p. 139.
318) "Theological Aphorisms," CQ, vol. 5, 1927, p. 54.
319) CQ, vol. 10, 1932, pp. 27-38.
320) Ibid., p. 39.
321) ETANT, p. 144.
322) "Theological Aphorisms," op.cit., p. 55.
323) ETANT, p. 144.
324) Religion in the Victorian Era, 1936, p. 272.
325) So that some have suggested that it took the tragedy of the First World W shatter liberal euphoria on the one hand, and to provide fertile soil for e Barthianism on the other.
326) ETANT, p. 19.
327) Ibid., p. 49.
328) CAS, p. 160.
329) Ibid., p. 166.
330) Ibid.
331) ETANT, p. 415.
332) Ibid., p. 124.
333) Ibid., p. 108.
334) Ibid., p. 86.
335) Ibid., p. 32.
336) T.W. Manson, The Teaching of Jesus, 2nd. ed., 1935, p. 300.
337) ETANT, p. 52.
338) "The Religion of the 'Shorter Catechism'," HR, Jan. 1927, p. 23.
339) ETANT, p. 104.
340) IRRS, p. 8.
341) Ibid., p. 9.
342) HTA, p. 15.
343) Ibid.
344) Ibid., and cf. "The Fact of the Atonement," ET, vol. 14, 1902-3, pp. 34
345) Ibid., p. 18.
346) Ibid., p. 23.
347) Ibid.
348) "The Theology of COPEC," HJ, vol. 23, 1924-5, p. 86.
349) HTA, p. 228, citing Moberly.
350) Ibid., pp. 228-9.
351) "The Fact of the Atonement," op.cit., p. 346.
352) Ibid.

A, p. 298.
ANT, p. 122.
e.g. ETANT, pp. 55-60.
I., p. 56.
A, p. 152.
I., p. 159.
ANT, p. 58.
I., pp. 423-4.
I., p. 424.
has just quoted Faber's lines:
ow Thou canst think so well of us, Yet be the God Thou art,
darkness to my intellect, But sunshine to my heart."
ie Fact of the Atonement," op.cit., p. 347.
I.
cent Thought on the Doctrine of the Atonement," ET, vol. 37, 1925-6,
199.
ie Fact of the Atonement," op.cit., p. 347.
. Hastings Rashdall.
loux was a Congregationalist.
view of The Message About the Cross, CQ, vol. 3, 1925, p. 249.
I., p. 250.
ie Fact of the Atonement," op.cit., pp. 349-350.
ANT, p. 303. Cf. CAS, p. 83.
A, pp. 154-5.
ie Religion of the "Shorter Catechism"," HR Jan. 1927, p. 21.
ANT, p. 69.
e.g. ETANT, p. 109.
I., p. 118. Cf. "Theological Aphorisms," CQ vol. 5, 1927, p. 56; and
ckintosh's particularly lucid article on "Universalism" in ed. J. Hastings,
Dictionary of Christ and the Gospels, vol. II, Edinburgh 1908, pp. 783-6.
I., p. 332.
p. 120.
S, p. 38.
CF, p. 46.
, p. 86.
I., p. 18.
ANT, p. 372. His CBK proceeds upon the assumption of "the trustworthiness
he moral consciousness, or the reality of the distinction between right and
ong." Op.cit., p. 7.
S, p. 152.
, p. 15.
p. 29. He elsewhere refers to "the Christian Socialist outlook, which declares
t love, mercy, generosity, is the whole of goodness; that Justice is infra-
ristian, and 'rights' inevitably 'selfish'; and, in brief, that Christ came into
world to found the Labour Party." "Recent Thought on the Doctrine of the
nement," ET, vol. 37, 1925-6, p. 203.
I., p. 30.

389) <u>V</u>, p. 31.
390) Ibid., pp. 43-44.
391) Ibid., pp. 47-8.
392) Ibid., p. 49.
393) We pass over a chapter on "Health as a Value," the burden of which is th should never be satisfied with health unbalanced by other values, nor con that because health is a value it should never be imperilled.
394) Ibid., p. 73.
395) Ibid., p. 94.
396) Ibid., p. 121.
397) "My Experiments in Authorship," <u>CQ</u>, vol. 9, 1931, p. 288.
398) <u>CAS</u>, pp. 211-212.
399) <u>HTA</u>, pp. 311-312. And cf. his criticisms of the COPEC Conference.
400) <u>PR</u>, p. 64.
401) <u>OWCF</u>, p. 52.
402) "Theism," <u>Encyc.Brit.</u> 11th ed. 1910-11, vol. 26, p. 755.
403) Ibid.
404) <u>HAH</u>, p. 5.
405) <u>CAS</u>, p. 131.
406) <u>CQ</u>, vol. 7, 1929, p. 113.
407) "Recent Thought on the Doctrine of the Atonement," <u>ET</u>, vol. 37, p. 200 note.
408) <u>ETANT</u>, p. 249.
409) <u>OWCF</u>, p. 48.
410) Ibid., p. 58.
411) <u>ETANT</u>, p. 475.

INDEX OF PERSONS AND PLACES

:n, 12, 28
  Walter Frederick, 23, 27, 94
s Magnus, 62
.er, Samuel, 28, 31, 95
, 62
, Thomas, 62, 63
er, 12
e, 63
ne of Hippo, 49
John, 60

John, 101
, Arthur James, 64
, 24
th, 31
Karl, 67
J. Vernon, 28
enjamin, 19, 22
, William Henry, 23, 94-95
y, George, 57
nann, Alois Emanuel, 71
;ham, 30, 94, 96
rn, Hugh, 14
W.G., 93
ridge, 14
Mass., 29
, Francis Herbert, 61
amily, 12
Annie: see Mackintosh, Annie
Robert, 13, 14
Alexander Balmain, 16, 18, 62
r, Johann Heinrich, 91
Joseph, 62, 63, 87

Cecil John, 76-77, 103
Edward, 14, 15, 24
John, 14, 55
I., 22
Anne: see McIntosh, Anne
Charles, 12
James, M., 26
John, 12
, Georg, 76

Calvary, 74, 76
Campbell, John McLeod, 87
Campbell, Lilias, 12
Candlish, James, 17
Candlish, R.S., 14
Cawdor, 12
Chalmers, Thomas, 91
Cobbe, Frances Power, 57
Comte, Auguste, 58
Condorcet, Marquis de, 71
Croy, 12

Darwin, Charles, 57, 58, 59
David, 88
Davidson, Andrew Bruce, 15, 93
Davidson, I. Hope, 22
Descartes, René, 57, 62
Didsbury, 19
Dods, Marcus, 16, 18
Douglas, John, 22
Drummond, Henry, 19
Duff, Archibald, 27, 95
Dumfries, 16, 19, 21-23
Dundee, 16
Dunoon, 12, 13, 92
Duns, John, 93

Edinburgh, 14, 15, 22
Edwards, Jonathan, 76
Elliott-Binns, L.E., 71
Elmslie, W.G., 16, 18
Emerson, Ralph Waldo, 25
Erskine, Thomas, of Linlathen, 92
Eucken, Rudolf C., 59
Ezra, 29

Faber, Frederick William, 103
Fairlie, 13, 14
Farries, Thomas C., 21
Fearn, 91
Ferguson, Joan, 31
Ferguson, Joseph, 31
Ferintosh, 12

105

Flew, A.G.N., 84
Flint, Robert, 63, 64, 101
Forsyth, Peter Taylor, 29
Fotheringham, A., 22
Fotheringham, R.A., 21
Fotheringham, R.P., 22
France, 16
Franks, Robert Sleightholme, 70

Garvie, Alfred Ernest, 27, 28, 57
Gethsemane, 76
Gibraltar, 92
Glasgow, 12, 14, 15, 22, 24
Goodrich, Albert, 25
Gough, Edward, 27
Gregory, James, 22
Grieve, Alexander James, 16, 23, 25, 29, 30, 33, 35, 95
Griffiths, H.P., 23
Grove, William Robert, 58

Halifax, 22
Harding, William Eric, 32
Hartlepool, 34
Hegel, Georg Wilhelm Friedrich, 26, 55, 59, 60-61, 63-64, 80, 87
Henley, William Ernest, 34
Herbert of Cherbury, Lord, 57
Herod, 88
Hickling, Charles Herbert, 23, 28
Hobbes, Thomas, 57
Hodge, Charles, 42
Holybourne, 92
Hooker, Richard, 55
Hume, David, 57, 63, 100
Huxley, Thomas Henry, 71

Irving, Miss, 22

James, Alfred Thomas Stephen, 31
James, Thomas Theophilus, 33
Jebb, Richard C., 14
Jena, 16
Jeremiah, 18
Jones, Henry, 14
Joule, James Prescott, 58

Kant, Immanuel, 60, 63, 64, 87
Keilah, 88
Kidd, Benjamin, 24, 58

Laughton, William, 54
Leibniz, Gottfried Wilhelm, 62
Lindsay, Thomas M., 17
Locke, John, 57, 63
London, 12
Lotze, Hermann, 69
Lushington, Edmund L., 14

Macgregor, James, 93
Mackennal, Alexander, 25
McKenzie, W. Douglas, 22
McKie, Miss, 22
Mackintosh, Aileen, 13
McIntosh, Angus, 12, 91
McIntosh, Anne, 12
Mackintosh, Annie, 13, 14, 16, 17,
Mackintosh, Charles Calder, 12, 1
Mackintosh, Elsie, 13
Mackintosh, Eneas, 13, 14, 92
Mackintosh, Janie, 13
Mackintosh, Jemima, 13
Mackintosh, Mary Wilson, 22-23, 2 33, 34
Mackintosh, Nan, 13
McLachlan, Samuel, 21
McTaggart, John McTaggart Ellis,
Manchester, 19, 22, 23, 24, 27, 31 34, 45, 55, 95
Manson, Thomas Walter, 72
Marburg, 16
Marple Bridge, 34
Martineau, James, 64
Melanchthon, Philipp, 91
Melrose, Andrew, 27
Micklem, Nathanael, 28, 96
Mill, John Stuart, 57, 64
Moberly, R.C., 49, 74
Moberly, W.H., 31, 32
Moody, Dwight L., 14, 36
Moore, George Edward, 84
Moxey, Anderson, 93
Mozley, John Kenneth, 88
Murphy, John, 33, 94

aland, 16, 92
John, 14

, Leonard Hulme, 26
John, 101
Herbert Howard, 33
Adolf, 101
John, 76
14, 96

e, 16
William, 62, 87
Mrs. G., 14
on, Howard, 29, 33
3, 50, 52, 65, 70, 73, 76
Arthur Samuel, 27, 28, 95
, George, 31, 96
Alexandria, 63
, Albert, 29

edt, Andreas, 76

Harry, 14
Robert, 14, 15, 16, 22, 27, 93
, Emily, 14
, George G., 14
l, Hastings, 69, 76
d of Sabunde, 101
homas, 59
s, John Slater, 25
Albrecht, 40, 71, 80
lary Wilson: see Mackintosh,
Wilson
ugh, 91
ames, 22
Josiah, 61
Bertrand Arthur William, 84

Ira D., 36

macher, Friedrich Daniel
t, 40
aleb, 23, 25, 94
?.J., 87-88
d, James Francis, 28
18
ge, Thomas, 21, 22, 23

Simon, David Worthington, 22, 94
Skye, 12
Smeaton, George, 93
Smeaton, Oliphant, 95
Smith, Walter, 16
Smith, William Robertson, 46
Socrates, 62
Spencer, Herbert, 58, 71
Spinoza, Baruch, 62
Strathdearn, 12
Sutherland, Duke of, 14

Tain, 12, 91, 92
Taxal, 33
Taylor, Alfred Edward, 61
Taylor, William, 92
Tennant, Hugh, 14
Theobald, Bernard Gage, 26, 32
Thompson, William (later Lord Kelvin), 14

Ure, George, 22
Urquhart: see Ferintosh

Veitch, John, 14

Watt, James, 21
Watts, Isaac, 99
Whaley Bridge, 23, 31, 33
Whyte, Alexander, 14, 15, 22
Wilkins, A.S., 25
Withington, 19, 23, 28, 31
Wolff, Christian, 63
Wright, W.M., 21, 23

www.ingramcontent.com/pod-product-compliance
Lightning Source LLC
Chambersburg PA
CBHW070943160426
43193CB00011B/1800